Denying the Truth
Revisiting *The X-Files* after 9/11

M. A. Crang

ISBN-13: 978-1517009038
ISBN-10: 1517009030

CONTENTS

INTRODUCTION

As I write this, production on the next chapter of *The X-Files* has now wrapped in Vancouver. A new "limited event series" will air in a few months' time in the early part of 2016. The teasers for these new instalments promise a return to the familiar territory of the series – with Mulder and Scully once again investigating unexplained phenomenon for the FBI. The brief glimpses released so far showcase *The X-Files'* signature visuals, stars Gillian Anderson and David Duchovny, along with the show's iconic theme music. These promotional spots are clearly designed to evoke nostalgic memories for the audience, many of whom grew up alongside these characters and this series.

Interestingly though, the teaser trailers also emphasise just how much the world has changed since the series first aired. Scully is shown taking a call from Mulder on her smartphone, instead of the usual 1990s 'brick' phone that we're accustomed to seeing. Mulder can also be heard railing against the spectre of ever-present government surveillance, noting that "we've never been in more danger." Anticipation for the series' return feels palpable, perhaps because concerns about the abuse of government power seem just as topical today as they did over two decades ago.

But while the zeitgeist now seems ready for a return to *The X-Files*, it wasn't always so. Towards the end of the show's broadcast, consensus was that society, and popular culture, had passed this series by. *The X-Files'* popularity had once crossed political and ideological boundaries. This show spoke to the audience's post-Cold War paranoia and anxieties so that, for a moment, it captured the world's attention. At some point though, the viewing environment changed… a terrible tragedy occurred which would forever change the world of the audience, but was scarcely acknowledged by the series itself. Following 9/11, the show's audience seemed to evaporate almost overnight. Many competing explanations have been offered for why *The X-Files* ended the way it did, but all tend to agree that by the time it concluded, the series was no longer culturally relevant.

Research for this book began several years ago, aiming to establish what it was that made the series so popular at its height. In many ways, it is impossible for us to know why an audience chooses to watch a particular text (or, for that matter, why they choose to stop watching). While 9/11 may not have featured prominently in the narrative of the series itself, this event has since become central to critical commentary about the show's production. What follows is not intended to be a definitive statement of the reasons for *The X-Files'* demise (the answer to that question depends entirely on the individual viewer), but it is hoped that it may at least contribute to the conversation.

This book is split into two parts: part one is a critical analysis of the text, examining the popular reception of the series and the possible effects of 9/11 on the show's audience. A wealth of academic and media commentary on *The X-Files* exists, from people far more qualified than I to comment on the show's reception. This section of the book draws on some of these opinions for a more complete reading of the series. While I am grateful to others who have gone before for their detailed research, any errors or omissions are my own. Mine is but one of a multitude of readings of a complex, multi-faceted series, and I fully expect some disagreement with my opinions. However, it is my hope that this book may at least prompt some readers to consider their own reasons for following this series so passionately.

Part two is more subjective – this section is simply a fan's 'musings' on each entry of *The X-Files* so far. These are not reviews in the traditional sense, but rather a brief impression of each instalment and its place within the series. These thoughts are offered only for those who may be curious to know the basis for the opinions expressed in part one. Given the opinions expressed in this book, it only seems fair to provide my personal views of the television series and the two feature films. This book is *not* intended as a comprehensive guide to the series, so my comments on each episode have been kept brief. It is perhaps inevitable, given the topic of this book, that slightly more attention has been paid to the later seasons. I have also assumed that readers have a working knowledge of *The X-Files*, so synopses are not included (a full episode list can be found in the appendix). Once again, I understand that many readers will disagree with my opinions on individual episodes. My own view of some entries has softened over time, while in the case of other episodes I remain as stubbornly against them as I was upon first viewing. My perspectives will surely continue to evolve in the future, but I hope that my views at this moment are of some passing interest to readers.

Fans of this series are notoriously passionate, sharing disagreements about many things. Was *The X-Files* defined by its overarching mythology, or the standalone episodes? Did it focus on Mulder's quest to find the truth, or Scully's journey from believer to sceptic? Was it about the central characters' relationship, or their professional investigations into the paranormal? A consensus on the answer to these questions will probably remain as elusive as ever in the future. But as we approach 2016, I think we can all agree that the prospect of new additions to *The X-Files* canon is surely a good thing.

M. A. Crang

Part I

The X-Files and 9/11

THE END OF AN ERA

On 10 September 1993, *The X-Files* first aired in the United States on the Fox network. As anyone familiar with the show would be aware, it followed the exploits of two FBI agents, Fox Mulder (David Duchovny) and Dana Scully (Gillian Anderson), in their investigations into the paranormal. Premiering in the final decade before the turn of the millennium, the series is now acknowledged by academics and critics alike as one of the most culturally resonant texts of its time. Many of these commentators cite the series' subject matter, and particularly its foregrounding of government conspiracies, aliens and other unexplained phenomena, as crucial to *The X-Files'* success. At the height of its popularity, *The X-Files* was the highest rating series on Rupert Murdoch's Fox network, regularly pulling in 20 million viewers in the U.S., while being broadcast in over 120 countries around the world. Despite this popular and critical acclaim, many analyses of the series neglect to acknowledge its ignominious end. The show eventually limped off the air due to dwindling ratings at the end of its ninth season. More recently, renewed interest in the series led to the announcement in March 2015 that *The X-Files* would be "rebooted," with a limited run of episodes to air on Fox in early 2016. While fans of the show await these new entries with keen anticipation, it seems an appropriate time to recall the circumstances in which the show concluded over a decade ago.

Before *The X-Files* ended in 2002, its audience had been in decline for several years. Few, however, could have expected the precipitous drop in ratings that occurred between the eighth and ninth seasons. Various theories have been put forward to explain why the show's popularity slumped so badly in the 2001/2002 season, with many noting that the premiere of the final season aired exactly two months after the terrorist attacks of 11 September 2001.

As with all aspects of life in the U.S., 9/11 had a dramatic impact on film and television. Many Hollywood productions were affected by these events, but while movie studios had time to recut and reschedule releases in the wake of the attacks, television was not afforded the same luxury. Production on *The X-Files'* ninth season was already well underway by September 2001. The series premiered only a short time later, ensuring that the ninth season went to air in a political and social environment that had changed profoundly from only a few months before. While production of the show was reportedly severely disrupted by the attacks, more importantly, the change in the zeitgeist that occurred after 9/11 has been cited as a major factor in the decision to end the series.

At the time of its cancellation, some suggested that the events of 9/11 had pushed *The X-Files* into "irrelevance," arguing that the series' concerns about sinister government machinations and alien colonisation were rendered moot in the face of such a tragedy. Others have pointed out that the series' depictions of a globalised world where governments could not be trusted were arguably *more* relevant in the wake of 9/11. Indeed, the series had presciently foreseen many of the issues that would dominate discussion in the post-9/11 world; including the encroachment of surveillance on civil liberties, and the need to limit executive power. In this regard, it is clear that the events of 9/11, occurring as they did so close to the premiere of *The X-Files'* final season, had an impact on the popular and critical reception of the show. After all, a key component of *The X-Files* was its emphasis on paranoia and government conspiracy.

When *The X-Files* premiered in September 1993, the post-Cold War environment was one in which questioning of government occurred freely. At that time, rather than being put off by any perceived criticism of authority, viewers were far more likely to be attracted to the series' basic premise that the government was not acting in their own best interests. As Executive Producer and series creator Chris Carter stated in 1995:

"We actually test marketed the show and what I was really surprised to learn was that everyone in the test audience believed that the government was not working in their best interests."[1]

This distrust of authority manifests itself in several ways in the series. From the very first episode, the protagonists are shown to be at odds with the very government that they supposedly represent. Upon being assigned to the "x-files," Scully is shocked to learn that her superiors expect her to 'debunk' Mulder's work. When the agents arrive at the site of their investigation, they find the town's sheriff and medical examiner to be hostile and uncooperative (a common thread throughout the series). Authority figures, like local law enforcement officers, are often depicted as selfish and petty on *The X-Files*, but the series suggests even more duplicitous motives on the part of the federal government. The conclusion to the pilot episode perfectly encapsulates this perspective – after Scully delivers her report, she presents her superiors with an implant, the only piece of physical evidence remaining from the investigation. This evidence is taken by the silent and nefarious Cigarette Smoking Man (William B. Davis) and stored in a labyrinthine vault in the base of the Pentagon. From its very beginnings therefore, the series suggests that the U.S. government does not want people to know the truth, and will take active steps to keep them from learning it. During the 1990s, this attitude clearly struck a chord with viewers.

---

[1] Denton, A. "*X-Files: An Investigation*" in *Rolling Stone*, Issue 517 (Yearbook 1995), pp. 67-74.

However, it appears that post-9/11 audiences' attitudes changed. The viewership that deserted the show in its final year was not seeking a subversive, challenging television text like *The X-Files*, which suggested that the government was actively engaged in a conspiracy to deceive the public. Instead, the terrible events of 9/11 led to a shift in the public consciousness, as the citizens of the U.S. looked to their leaders in government for solace. It is hardly coincidental that George W. Bush, a President who would plumb the depths of popularity for much of his time in office, saw his approval rating skyrocket immediately after 9/11. While the President's popularity had been in general decline just prior to the attacks, following 9/11 the U.S. public unquestioningly fell in behind their leaders, with the active encouragement of certain sections of the media (in particular, Rupert Murdoch's cable network, Fox News).

It is in this context that this book will seek to engage with the question of whether or not the massive socio-political changes that accompanied 9/11 extended as far as the population's television viewing habits. Specifically, this book will assess whether or not *The X-Files'* audience, weary of stories of government conspiracy and cover-up, switched stations in favour of television texts that reaffirmed their faith in authority.

Serial vs Series
A basic knowledge of the series' structure is beneficial in order to understand its reception by the audience. *The X-Files* generally presented two types of stories; standalone episodes focusing on a single, self-contained investigation into supernatural phenomena such as the occult, psychics or genetic mutants, and the mythology episodes which looked at the continuing government conspiracy to conceal the truth about extraterrestrials. Film and television scholars generally identify two predominant televisual formats – the 'serial' and the 'series'. However, by splitting its episodes into two discrete types, *The X-Files* blurs this distinction.

The show's standalone episodes were essentially genre stories in which Mulder and Scully investigated strange phenomena in their role as FBI agents. Cast and crew of the show occasionally referred to these episodes as the 'monster of the week' stories, because the antagonist changed from week to week, never to reappear again. On rare occasions, particularly popular antagonists were brought back for a return appearance in subsequent episodes. For example, Eugene Tooms, a stretching, liver eating mutant, appeared in two episodes during the show's first season. Likewise, the third season character of 'Pusher,' who is able to force his will onto others, returned for an encore in season five. Overwhelmingly though, the standalone investigations were self-contained, requiring little knowledge of events that had gone before, and offering some degree of narrative closure (albeit limited, as we shall see). The standalone episodes therefore adhere to the definition of a 'series' in that the characters remain static in different situations. While the formats may recur each week, the characters generally lose all memory of the preceding events so that each episode feels fresh.

But as a television text, *The X-Files* does not strictly adhere to this definition of a 'series.' Throughout its run (but in particular from the second season onwards), the show also contained a narrative arc following Mulder and Scully's efforts to expose an increasingly elaborate government conspiracy. Characters in these stories would reappear, and the audience's understanding of these events required a knowledge of what had gone before. Therefore the mythology episodes closely resemble the 'serial' or 'soap' form, in that the narrative develops over time; characters remember and events accumulate as "a slow history."[2]

Although the breakdown between standalone and mythology episodes was roughly equal, commentary on the show has tended to prioritise the series' main mythology arc. This book will focus on *both* the standalone and mythology episodes to argue that the

---

[2] For a detailed summary of both formats, see: Ellis, J. *Visible Fictions: Cinema, Television, Video*, Routledge, London/New York, 1982, pp. 147, 157.

show presented a subversive and inflammatory political perspective. While the mythology storyline may have featured express criticism of government, we will see that even the series' stand-alone episodes, with their connections to the Gothic horror tradition, served to question social and political authority.

Trust No One

The first section of this book will demonstrate that *The X-Files* presented a political and ideological perspective of the U.S. government that would have proven unpalatable post-9/11. Although some characterise the series as inflammatory and rebellious because of its paranoid content, others have argued just as stridently that the series is not radical at all. Indeed, it is questionable whether a show as commercially successful as *The X-Files* could ever *truly* question authority. Ultimately though, it will be shown that the show actively encouraged its audience to question the institution of government through both its style and content. Therefore the politics of *The X-Files* would undoubtedly have had a profound impact on the audience's decision to tune out after the shock of an event as momentous as 9/11.

Believe The Lie

Beyond the show's politics, a related consideration is whether or not the series presented itself as a 'real' text. Despite the fantastic nature of the stories presented, *The X-Files* lay claims to authenticity by setting its narrative within a recognisably real world. Obviously if the show is perceived as being realistic, or at least possible, then the influence of the series' political position would be heightened. By encouraging the audience to identify with the world in which the series is set, and taking steps to connect this setting with real-life events, *The X-Files* may be able to effect the audience's perception of their own reality. It will be demonstrated that the series' setting within a world that was similar to (if not the same) as its audience, served to heighten the program's subversive political message. In this sense, *The X-Files'* claims to realism were seen as too frightening, too close to home, following 9/11.

Deny Everything

A blurring of the boundaries between reality and fiction is considered to be one of the main features of post-modernism. While *The X-Files* is often categorised as part of the 'science-fiction' genre, the show's creators have rejected this label. At the time of its broadcast, the producers of *The X Files* emphasised the credibility of the show's stories, frequently stating that the narrative dealt with 'extreme possibility.' Chris Carter actively encouraged comparisons between the show's storylines and reality, stating in 1996 that:

> *"The idea that there are bad people out there working in dark and shadowy ways outside the system, I think, is very believable and real."*[3]

This book will posit that *The X-Files* was narratively and televisually a post-modern series that blurred the boundary between real-life fact and the series' fiction. Citing specific examples, it will be demonstrated that this blurring of boundaries, along with the program's verisimilitude and subversive political tone, could potentially have a direct impact on the audience's interpretation of their own reality.

Everything Dies

The final section of this book will examine the reception of *The X-Files* from viewers and critics. As with any example of popular culture, numerous reasons have been cited for why the program's viewership vanished in its final year. While it will be argued that the series' demise was *primarily* attributable to 9/11, production of the show did not remain static between its penultimate year and its ninth season. *The X-Files* evolved radically in its final years as a result of changes to its cast, its shooting location, and simply the length of time it had remained on the air. Each of these changes will be examined in detail, along with their impact on the series' reception.

---

[3] Wild, D. "*X-Files*: Undercover" in *Rolling Stone*, Issue 524 (July 1996), pp. 54-58, 97.

Ultimately, despite the many arguments which have been made for the failure of *The X-Files'* last season to find an audience, the most compelling explanation for the series' drop in popularity is cultural – a change in the zeitgeist precipitated by the 9/11 terrorist attacks. With the benefit of being able to consider the entirety of *The X-Files'* canon, it is clear that the show was a product of the pre-millennial, Clinton-era of the 1990s. The events of 9/11, signalling as they did massive shifts within U.S. and Western society, culture and politics, ultimately brought about the end of the series' cultural moment. *The X-Files* flourished in an environment where authority could be openly questioned, while fiction and reality were blurred. The strength of *The X-Files* was its ability to make viewers wonder about 'the truth' that was supposedly out there. However it will be established that after 11 September 2001, those same viewers rejected the series' truth in favour of one which did not implore them to question authority. After the trauma of 9/11, a majority of *The X-Files'* viewers no longer wanted to believe, and deserted the show for something more palatable to them.

TRUST NO ONE
THE POLITICS OF *THE X-FILES*

During its broadcast, significant debate was devoted to determin-
ing whether *The X-Files* occupied the left or right of the political
spectrum. However, discussion of the show's *perceived* political
leanings is ultimately less helpful than analysing its depiction of
the institution of government itself. This approach can best be
summed up by the following statement from Chris Carter to
Rolling Stone in 1996:

> *"People say the show is obviously Republican because it says
> government is a bad thing. I think Republicans say, 'Trust <u>us</u>.' And I'm
> saying, 'Trust <u>no one</u>.'"*[4]

Rather than asking whether or not 9/11 contributed to the end of
The X-Files, it is equally valid to suggest that the show itself was a
product of the Clinton-era and that its audience disappeared with
the passing of that period. Though most people can easily quan-
tify the simple notion of "post-9/11" (by virtue of the fact that it
refers to a specific event and date); the Clinton-era does not just
refer to Bill Clinton's presidency, but to a specific historical time
period. What do we mean then when we talk of the "Clinton-era"?

---

[4] Chris Carter quoted in: Wild, D. "X-Files: Undercover" in *Rolling Stone*, Issue 524 (July 1996), p. 58.

Towards the end of the Cold War, tensions between the West and the Soviet Union were revived under President Ronald Reagan. It is generally acknowledged that film and television echoed the sentiments of the country during the Reagan presidency by becoming more conservative. Reagan was unique as a President in that he himself had been a Hollywood actor before entering politics. This legacy can be seen in Reagan's appropriation of the language of fictional 1980s heroes like Rambo, and his famous description of the U.S.S.R. as the "evil empire" (borrowed from *Star Wars*). Following Reagan, George Bush Sr., another Republican president, continued this trend of reviving U.S. nationalism. Unlike his predecessor, Bush had no historical connection with Hollywood. In his most notorious attack on the entertainment industry, Bush declared to the Annual Convention of the National Religious Broadcasters that, "we need a Nation closer to *The Waltons* than *The Simpsons*." This attitude to television programs which were deemed by the moral majority to be unwholesome or subversive (such as *The Simpsons*) characterised 'network era television,' when television texts focused on old-fashioned family values and generally promoted trust in established authorities.

Following the collapse of communism and the end of the Cold War, Bush was succeeded by the Democratic President Bill Clinton. As well as bringing great political change, the swearing in of the Clinton administration is also said to have heralded the arrival of cult TV texts, such as *The X-Files*. In place of the old certainties that had existed during the Cold War, the Clinton-era has been described as ushering in "New World Disorder."[5] This new world was characterised by the breaking down of the traditional 'us' and 'them' barriers which had previously existed, and *The X-Files* reflects this chaos and disorder. As trust and confidence in the institutions of U.S. society waned, the public felt more free to openly criticise the structures that had been established to perpetuate

---

[5] For further information, see: Reeves, J. L., Rodgers, M. C. & Epstein, M. "Rewriting Popularity: The Cult Files" in *Deny All Knowledge* (Ed. David Lavery, Angela Hague and Marla Cartwright), Syracuse University Press, Syracuse, 1996, pp. 22-35.

dominant ideologies. With the downfall of the Soviet Union, the U.S. appeared to have defeated the last of its enemies as the millennium drew to a close. In the absence of external enemies and shocked by government abuses of power, like Watergate and the Iran-Contra scandal, Americans' attention in the 1990s turned to consider the possibility that internal enemies could threaten their future. The 1995 bombing of a federal office building in Oklahoma City demonstrated that, for some at least, foremost among these internal enemies was the U.S. government.

New World Disorder
In such an environment, the popularity of *The X-Files* during the 1990s was not simply serendipitous or coincidental. In season four's "Musings of a Cigarette Smoking Man," the dramatised resignation of Gorbachev and the collapse of communism are greeted by a bureaucrat observing that the U.S. is now without "enemies." This becomes a recurring theme, with the series recognising that post-Cold War America is no longer bound by the same political consensus that had existed earlier. In fact, *The X-Files'* emergence during the Clinton-era can be seen not only as a reaction to the *end* of the Cold War, but a response to the *beginning* of a world no longer characterised by the same political certainties. With U.S. citizens no longer able to identify a recognisable 'other' threatening their peaceful existence, political leaders struggled to convince a sceptical public of their good intentions. Very often, this scepticism was given voice in *The X-Files*. In the second season episode, "Red Museum," a Wisconsin farmer suggests that growth hormones injected into cattle could be responsible for the strange and sometimes violent behaviour of the town's young people. When Scully protests that the Food & Drug Administration has assured consumers that the hormones are safe, the farmer scoffs at her blind faith in the "government." Such examples clearly demonstrate the public distrust of authority that pervaded American society before 9/11.

In this way, *The X-Files* clearly represents the Clinton-era, where government was not to be trusted, and the populace's response to their leaders' authority became increasingly cynical. The series' emergence as a television phenomenon took place at the very moment when the West (and particularly the U.S.) began to intro-spectively wonder about the consequences of the unrestrained growth of military and governmental power that had occurred since World War II. This introspection manifests itself in the se-ries' explicit questioning of governmental authority, as *The X-Files* frequently criticises the U.S. government in ways that earlier tele-vision series had not. For a show with such a radical perspective, it is instructive to analyse the series' depictions of government and authority before 9/11 (an event with far-reaching social and political consequences).

"The 'I' in F.B.I."

From its inception, *The X-Files* displays as suspicious and un-trustworthy the government institutions supposedly charged with protecting ordinary citizens. In one of the program's first scenes, Scully is charged with the dubious assignment of 'debunking' Mulder's work by her superiors, the sinister and taciturn Cigarette Smoking Man among them. In this way, *The X-Files* depicts the apparatus of executive government, represented by monolithic bureaucracies like the FBI, as cold and impersonal.

Some argue that by having the protagonists serve as federal offi-cers, *The X-Files* actually casts government in a positive light. It has been argued that the series is not subversive at all, given that a conscious decision was made to cast its main protagonists as gor-geous, youthful, intelligent agents of the Federal Bureau of Inves-tigation.[6] While the agency itself may be called into question, Mulder and Scully are always depicted as the series' touchstones – exposing corruption, solving the mystery and bringing the perpetrators to justice. Indeed, Chris Carter stated in interviews at

---

[6] For example, see: Haggins, B.L. "Apocrypha Meets *The Pentagon Papers:* The Appeals of *The X-Files* to the X-Phile" in *Journal of Film and Video*, Vol. 53, No. 4 (Winter 2001/02), pp. 8-28.

the time of the show's broadcast that he was invited to the Bureau's Washington headquarters for an unofficial tour; "We got nice treatment from the agents who were big fans of the show. They think it has shed a good light on the FBI."[7]

With the series having now ended, the FBI's role within the context of *The X-Files* storylines and politics has arguably become clearer. While the series does call into question the FBI's role as an institution of government, *The X-Files* ultimately depicts the Bureau as an intermediary of a shadow government that exercises control over Mulder and Scully's superiors from afar. Although this was hinted at throughout the series, it is first explicitly stated in the fifth season premiere, "Redux." In this episode, Mulder describes to Scully how the cancer she has been diagnosed with and an elaborate hoax on the American people have direct connections back to the FBI. Similarly in the sixth season premiere, "The Beginning," the agents' confidant within the Bureau, Assistant Director Walter Skinner (Mitch Pileggi), pleads with Mulder that he cannot pressure or argue with the members of a conspiracy who walk the FBI's halls with "absolute impunity." Examples such as these present the FBI as a sinister and repressive force, unaccountable to the people, and uncontrollable due to its size and influence.

Despite *The X-Files'* apparent willingness to paint the FBI as a cold, unfeeling institution of a powerful government, it must be remembered that the characters at the heart of the show are officers of this executive agency. The contradiction between the agents' quest to reveal government misdeeds, while simultaneously working as agents of the government that is out to get them, is a fundamental tenet of the series. Agents Mulder and Scully frequently come across abuses of power by government agencies, but their own authority to conduct these investigations is derived from that same government.

---

[7] Chris Carter quoted in: Wild, D. "X-Files: Undercover" in *Rolling Stone*, Issue 524 (July 1996), p. 58.

The X-Files' later entries arguably suffered from the loss of this dichotomy between the character's quest to uncover government involvement in conspiracies, and Scully and Mulder's duty to the federal government as their employer. In the eighth season episode, "Vienen," Mulder's employment with the FBI is officially terminated. From this moment on, Mulder is no longer able to conduct official investigations into the paranormal. Perhaps understandably, *The X-Files'* writers struggled to deal with the character's loss of authority. For example, the secret military tribunal convened for Mulder's trial in "The Truth" – described as a hearing for the "agent" by his own "agency" – stretches the viewer's logic as much as any of the series' paranormal storylines. The entire premise of the series' final episode conveniently ignores the fact that Mulder has already been dismissed by the Bureau. Having lost any authority to act on behalf of the FBI, it strains credulity to believe that his former employer would be actively involved in any trial.

Mulder's loss of authority is painfully depicted in the second feature film, *I Want to Believe*, which opens with the character unshaven, apparently unemployed, and collecting newspaper clippings on paranormal phenomena. Scully and Mulder are then asked to assist the FBI with a missing person investigation (in an apparent acknowledgement that without any official mandate, Mulder's character resembles just another paranoid crackpot). Unable to derive any official power from the FBI to conduct his investigations, Mulder loses a crucial part of his character's identity. Indeed, when he confronts the antagonists in the film's conclusion (armed only with a wrench), Mulder's character is displayed as frustratingly impotent – even before he is quickly knocked unconscious. In the end, his rescue must be effected by Skinner, who still works with the Bureau. As a result, we see that Mulder and Scully's positions as officers of the very government that they were seeking to investigate formed a crucial dichotomy within the series.

Perhaps the most definitive statement of FBI complicity in government crimes occurs in the series' final instalment, "The Truth." During the episode, first broadcast on 19 May 2002, Mulder is accused of murdering a soldier at a secret government facility. When Mulder's former superior, FBI Deputy Director Kersh (James Pickens Jr.), discusses the situation with his military counterpart, Kersh is ordered to conduct Mulder's trial in a military court because the General wants a guilty verdict. It is interesting to note the spectre of the Guantanamo Bay detention of terrorist suspects, which had begun only months earlier in January 2002, as Kersh presciently observes that the proposed hearing appears to be outside the boundaries of the law. These concerns are dismissed by the military General, who ominously states that the government is now run by forces that are too dangerous to defy. With a look of resigned acceptance, the FBI Deputy Director then reluctantly agrees. This scene demonstrates that the FBI itself is not the supreme villain on *The X-Files*. The villain is the all-powerful shadow government that directs these organs of authority and the individuals within them. The Bureau is presented as powerless to defend itself against encroachments from this insidious conspiracy.

The Syndicate: The 'Shadow Government'
The notion of a shadow government, operating beyond the political sphere occupied by citizens themselves, is the logical extension of the series' preoccupation with presenting the institution of government as unaccountable. The democratic order in *The X-Files* is subverted by the existence of an unelected, all-powerful, secret cabal which wields *true* power. For example, when one of the Cigarette Smoking Man's lackeys asks whether or not the President should be advised of their plans, the Cigarette Smoking Man's response is to observe that the President should not even know that people like him exist. This line confirms that the democratically elected government – apparently of the people, by the people and for the people – is so separate from the shadow government that the two can never co-exist. In this sense, the

series depicts the institutions of government, such as the FBI, as powerless to stop abuses of power by the *institution of government* itself.

Therefore, *The X-Files* subverts popular American notions of democracy and the separation of powers in its depiction of authority – the shadow government (or "Syndicate" as it is known on the series) occupies all levels of power and is able to manipulate public agencies to do its bidding. It is interesting to note that in the wake of 9/11 this was an idea that gained some mainstream political currency with left-leaning commentators critical of the influence of Dick Cheney. Following concerns about the undemocratic nature of the 2000 election, which was ultimately decided by the United States Supreme Court, the Vice-President to George W. Bush was frequently cast as the 'puppet-master' behind government policies, including the decision to send America to war in Iraq. The most explicit accusation that Cheney operated beyond the power granted to the office of Vice President came following 9/11, when it emerged that after the terrorist attacks he had travelled to a secret government facility with other bureaucrats where, some argue, he momentarily became the leader a U.S. 'shadow government.'[8] These real-world parallels between the storylines of *The X-Files* and contemporary American politics were invariably forwarded by left-leaning opponents of the then Republican government, raising the question of whether or not *The X-Files* does in fact present a partisan political agenda?

As Chris Carter has admitted, some have accused the series of being a haven for right-wing paranoia during the 1990s. When a federal office building in Oklahoma City was bombed on 19 April 1995 – exactly two years after the deadly fire that ended the siege in Waco, Texas – some indirectly connected these events to *The X-Files*. For example, some have argued that the series' insistence that, "Government denies knowledge" (an aphorism that appears

---

[8] For example, see: Scott, P. D. *The Road to 9/11: Wealth, Empire, and the Future of America*, University of California Press, Berkley, 2007, p. 237.

In every episode of the series bar the pilot) encourages anti-government paranoia. This view of the show equates the series' depiction of government with traditional right-wing opposition to 'big' government.[9]

In contrast to those who see the show as occupying the right of the political spectrum, others see *The X-Files* as leftist because of this same distrust of authority. We have already seen that the series places a great emphasis on the collapse of the traditional 'us' and 'them' distinctions that existed during the Cold War. Accordingly, some have speculated that by demonising the military and the establishment, the series presents a left-wing perspective that is uniquely linked to the administration of Bill Clinton.[10] What is interesting about these perspectives is that *The X-Files* is read as either left or right wing for the same reasons – the series' representation of government.

Whilst there is almost unanimous agreement that *The X-Files* is critical of government, arguably the most accurate assessment of the series' politics present the show as occupying the middle-ground. Although both right and left-wing commentators apparently identify with the series' political viewpoint, the show studiously avoids any appearance of partisanship. The series does not advocate any particular ideological viewpoint, and accordingly appeals to audiences on either side of the political divide. Mulder and Scully's primary antagonists are not elected officials (of Republican or Democratic stripes) but a shadow government that is ultimately answerable to no one. Furthermore, by presenting the show's protagonists as FBI agents, *The X-Files* manages to tread a fine line between paranoid criticism of government, and veneration of government authorities.

---

[9] For example, see: Neumann, A.W. "*The X-Files* and the Longing for Belief" in *Quadrant*, Vol. 40, No. 9 (September 1996), pp. 23-27.

[10] For example, see: Kaye, H. "Fin-de-Siècle Fears: *The X-Files* as Contemporary Gothic" in *Fictions of Unease: The Gothic from Otranto to The X-Files* (Ed. Andrew Smith, Diane Mason and William Hughes), Sulis Press, Newton Park, 2002, pp. 202-210.

When considering the impact of 9/11 on the series, a fundamental question is whether or not *The X-Files'* representation of government is actually subversive. Does the series undermine people's belief in authority, or not? The show clearly strains to present itself as subversive – employing aphorisms like "Fight the Future," "Resist or Serve" and "Deny Everything," ostensibly to attack the established order. But the show also attacks the established order in other, more subtle ways. While this analysis has so far focused on the series' mythology episodes, those that explicitly dramatise government misdeeds and conspiracies, *The X-Files'* standalone genre stories are equally subversive.

The Subversive Gothic Tradition
The X-Files has frequently been associated with the Gothic because of its horrific, supernatural, and occasionally macabre subject matter. But this is not the series' only connection with the genre - Gothic texts also represent a challenge to the intellectual and moral status quo. In this sense, the term 'Gothic' does not just describe a literary genre, but a libertarian political ideology. The political dimension of the Gothic has its basis in English history and the 'Gothic constitution' of 1688. According to some Englishmen, fundamental principles of liberty stretched back to ancient Germanic people, which went on to be fostered and developed within England. Similarly, the notion of 'elective monarchy,' which refutes the divine right of royalty and rejects tyranny, has its origins within the Gothic.

It is therefore clear that the Gothic functions as a subversive literary genre. Just as classic Gothic literature and ideology questioned authority, so too does *The X-Files* represent a contemporary iteration of the genre. The series echoes the genre implicitly through its style and tone, and explicitly through its content. By presenting stories involving satanic rituals, psychic manipulation, shape-shifting human beings, and ghostly apparitions, *The X-Files* directly connects itself to the Gothic and continues this tradition of challenging the status quo.

By framing its narrative against an official backdrop, where these strange occurrences are worthy of official investigation by the authorities and characters like Mulder legitimise the surrounding discourse with convincing, pseudo-scientific jargon, *The X-Files* presents a world in which the dominance of institutional authority and science is questioned. In the Clinton-era, just as the series' audience expressed cynicism at their political leaders' claims of honesty, many also shared a pre-millennial distrust of science and rationality. Indeed, sceptics pilloried the series at the height of its popularity, arguing that its depictions of paranormal phenomena and fantastic narratives influenced the audience's perceptions of the world around them. One high-profile example of this was the atheist Richard Dawkins, who wrote at the time of its broadcast that *The X-Files* was "anti-rational." For him, the high-profile of the series, and the legitimacy with which it presented its fantastic stories, combined to form an "insidious" obstacle to logical thinking.[11] In this way, the series explicitly continues the Gothic tradition of challenging science's infallibility, in a similar manner to Gothic authors such as Mary Shelley.

Separate from the mythology episodes' arguably explicit attacks on the institution of government, *The X-Files'* standalone episodes can also be viewed within this destabilizing Gothic tradition that criticised the dominant social order. Gothic stories, such as Shelley's *Frankenstein; or, The Modern Prometheus* (in which the eponymous doctor's experiments interfere with the natural order) exposed the fallibility of the individuals wielding political, scientific or social power. *The X-Files* quite clearly updates these notions of the abuse of scientific power, depicting genetic manipulation and advances in technology as something to be feared rather than celebrated. For example, consider the early episode, "Eve," in which the agents investigate separate murders where two men were mysteriously drained of blood. Although Mulder initially suspects the involvement of aliens, the killers are

---

[11] Dawkins, R. *Unweaving the Rainbow: Science, Delusions, and the Appetite for Wonder*, Mariner Books, New York, 1998, p. 28.

later revealed to be the victims' daughters – genetically modified clones, resulting from a failed experiment to create a superior soldier. This narrative depicts scientific power being exploited for nefarious means and, as with so many Gothic stories, the hubris of those conducting these experiments lies in their misguided belief that they can control nature.

The show also depicts examples of abuses of power by modern office-holders, reworking the Gothic archetypes of nobles or monks for the modern day – such as the lawyer who suppresses evidence in "Redrum," or the doctor who murders his patients in "Sanguinarium." For much of its run, the show's stories also took place within that favoured Gothic setting; dreary, moonlit forests. Similarly, the Antarctic conclusion to The X-Files' first feature film, Fight the Future, appears to owe a significant debt to another Gothic-inspired story, H.P. Lovecraft's At The Mountains of Madness. But the series does not simply recreate Gothic iconography – instead it adapts and updates these motifs for the present, with labyrinthine government facilities substituting for the traditional settings of Gothic fiction. Accordingly, we can see that The X-Files reiterates its overt attacks on the institution of government by adhering to the Gothic tradition of undermining established authority. Quite apart from the show's overt political commentary, the series' narrative similarity to the Gothic clearly distinguishes it as subversive.

But some argue that monsters and occult imagery are simply employed to suppress dissent and reinforce established authorities. According to this viewpoint, these stories only serve to legitimise institutional authority by depicting police or military forces as protection against such threats.[12] Ultimately however, the ambiguous endings which characterise The X-Files serve only to further undermine these dominant societal forces. Indeed, by the end of many episodes, the narrative is not adequately explained.

---

[12] For example, see Kellner, D. "The X-Files and the Aesthetics and Politics of Postmodern Pop" in The Journal of Aesthetics and Art Criticism, Vol. 57, No. 2 (Spring 1999), pp. 161-175.

For example, "Genderbender" depicts a killer who is able to alter their gender. In appropriately Gothic fashion, Mulder and Scully's investigations lead them to an isolated and reclusive community known as the Kindred, whose members know the killer as "Brother Martin." Eventually, Brother Martin is discovered at the site of another murder, only for the Kindred to materialise out of thin air to secret him away. Returning to the Kindred's village, the agents find the buildings abandoned, with only a few crop circles left as evidence of any previous inhabitants. No explanation is offered for the killer's ability to change sexes, the mysterious crop circles or the Kindred's ability to appear out of nowhere (and disappear just as quickly). Admittedly, this episode is an extreme example, but what it demonstrates is the open-ended nature of *The X-Files'* storytelling.

Another device the series employs repeatedly is for the agents to dispatch the perceived threat, only for it to reappear before the end credits. For example, season two's "The Host" deals with a giant, sewer dwelling, mutant fluke worm born out of the contamination of the Chernobyl disaster. The story ends with Agent Mulder apparently killing the fluke by slicing it in two with a metal sewer grate. However, the final lingering shot of the fluke's carcass shows it floating in the sewer... and slowly opening its eyes. This narrative device was used so often by the series that, in later seasons, the producers began to worry that it may have become too familiar. The sixth season episode, "Alpha," was to have ended with a shot suggesting that the episode's monster (an extinct dog known as the *wanshang dhole*) had survived. This scene was ultimately omitted late in production, with writer Frank Spotnitz commenting on the DVD release that the original ending, "felt like something we had done many times before on *The X-Files*."[13]

---

[13] This quote is transcribed from the "Deleted Scenes" special feature on the sixth season DVD release: *The X-Files: The Complete Sixth Season*, Region 4, Disc 6, Twentieth Century Fox Home Entertainment, 2002, DVD.

This demonstrates how inconclusive finality became a feature of the series, with episodes frequently defying resolution and leaving questions unanswered. In this sense, *The X-Files'* standalone episodes do not legitimate authority figures like the FBI at all – Mulder and Scully's credentials are depicted as powerless to confront the disorder which characterises their world, as well as our own.

Mainstream Subversion

Some have queried how *The X-Files* achieved commercial success despite its paranoid conspiracy themes. In fact, as we have seen, much of the series' success can arguably be attributed to its politically subversive tone. Before concluding any discussion of the series' politics though, it should be emphasised that the text itself is a commercial entity. Following the enormous success of the show, an array of products were released bearing *The X-Files'* brand. Amongst the plethora of merchandising to emerge from the show, *The X-Files* would go on to spawn numerous official and unofficial guide books, several tie-in comics, computer games, collectible trading cards, numerous novel adaptations and the obligatory home video releases.

In addition to the revenue raised by the series' merchandising, much has been made of *The X-Files'* syndication on the News Corporation-owned FX cable network in the US, where it became the highest rating program following its debut in 1997. The series was syndicated for a record $600,000 per episode, but David Duchovny sued 20th Century Fox during production of the seventh season claiming an alleged $25 million in unpaid royalties. The actor claimed that by transferring the syndication rights to the Fox network's cable affiliate, the studio had received less than if the rights had been sold on the open market. The claim was eventually settled out of court before production of the show's penultimate season began. [14]

---

[14] Flint, J, "It's Fox vs Fox" in *Entertainment Weekly*, Issue 501 (3 Sep 1999), pp.15-16.

A 1998 estimate found that for News Corporation, the series would generate a profit of around $1.4 billion to $1.5 billion "over the expected eight-season life of the show."[15] While undoubtedly impressive, this sizeable estimate neglects several key contributors to *The X-Files*' overall profitability. Firstly, the series eventually ran for *nine* seasons rather than eight, along with two feature films (the upcoming six episode 'limited event series' scheduled for 2016 will only add to this syndication catalogue). Indeed, a key motivator for Fox in opting to revive the property would clearly have been the value of licensing the show to streaming services, such as Netflix and Amazon. While such distribution avenues were unheard of at the time of the series' original broadcast, their arrival has only added to the show's profitability for News Corporation, allowing the series to continue generating revenue long after its original broadcast.

Just as importantly, many estimates of the show's profitability during its broadcast would have omitted the eventual revenue gained from the DVD box-sets of the series (and their inevitable reissues). Along with other new media, the DVD box-set contributed to the decline in traditional television audiences by providing consumers with the ability to enjoy their favourite television programming at their leisure, freed from the constraints of cumbersome scheduling or intrusive advertisements. Not coincidentally, the DVD box-set was pioneered by News Corporation in its continued efforts to merchandise and commodify *The X-Files*. Although they are now ubiquitous, the first ever DVD box-set was the release of the first season of *The X-Files* in April 2000. According to a Fox spokesperson speaking before the premiere of the 2008 feature film, the series had sold $600 million worth of DVDs worldwide (a number that will only have grown in intervening years).[16]

---

15 Roberts, J.L. "TV Turns Vertical" in *Newsweek*, Vol. 132, Iss. 16 (19 October 1998), p. 54.
16 Kaufman, A. "An 'X-Files' Mystery; Film Will Reveal Whether Fox Can Revive Aging Cult Favorite" in *The Wall Street Journal* (Easter Edition), New York, 25 July 2008, p. B12.

How then can a commercial series such as *The X-Files* present a dissident political view, when its very success – and continued survival – depends so heavily on the mainstream political imperatives of capitalism and rampant consumerism? It is easy to dismiss *The X-Files'* claims of resistance to political authority purely by virtue of its astounding popularity – top-rating network television series arguably define the status quo, rather than subvert it. In this way, the series can become a disposable object for its viewers, who watch in order to experience the *illusion* of subversion, without actually changing their behaviour towards government or authority. According to this reading, in order for a text to be *truly* subversive it must somehow galvanise its viewers towards political engagement. But to hold any popular film and television text to this high standard is arguably unrealistic. Admittedly, *The X-Files* straddles a fine line between the unorthodox political content of the text itself, and the mainstream processes by which it is marketed, but ultimately this does not compromise the clear subversive tendencies of the series' narrative.

BELIEVE THE LIE
REALISM IN *THE X-FILES*

The question of 'realism' within television has existed for as long as the medium itself. Some theorists argue that mass media has lost all meaning for contemporary audiences to the extent that they need no longer distinguish between reality and fiction – the boundaries between the two having become so blurred that the distinction is now irrelevant.

With reference to *The X-Files*, this suggests that the politically subversive vision presented by the show may become indistinguishable from actual fact. Television is a particularly potent medium because the audience's degree of exposure is heightened compared to the cinema – television series often last for several years, and they may continue to be broadcast decades after they were first produced. This affords television series, like *The X-Files*, far more capacity than other media to influence the lives of their audience.

Several episodes of *The X-Files* expressly deal with the increasingly pervasive presence of electronic media in people's lives. For example, "Blood" depicts normally sane people being pushed over the edge by subliminal messages from their home appliances. However, perhaps the most explicit comment the series has made on television's ability to palpably represent reality occurs in "Wetwired," where a scrambled television signal induces paranoid hallucinations. Exposure to this signal causes Scully to turn on Mulder, believing him to be a member of the government conspiracy. This storyline is apparently a tongue-in-cheek response to those who argue that excessive exposure to television inevitably damages the audience. But in presenting examples of television viewers who are unable to distinguish between reality and their own television-induced hallucinations, the series is also commenting on the power of the medium to define the world of the audience. Having already concluded that the series presents a critique of authority, and particularly the institution of government, it is instructive to consider the effect that such a critique could have on an audience that may no longer be able to distinguish between reality and artifice. It is clear that the effect would be an intensification of the series' subversive message – to "trust no one" – and further, that this message would have proven unwelcome for audiences immediately following 9/11.

This is not to suggest that *The X-Files'* audience mistakes the series' dramatised stories for actual reality. Others have sought to claim that the series contributed to an increasing suggestibility in society. For example, *Skeptic* magazine stated that increased belief in conspiracy theories in contemporary society is to be expected from, "a generation raised on the *X-Files*."[17] Similarly, some have argued that the series' popularity is evidence of the gullibility of the American public, who apparently accept the series' stories at face value and cannot distinguish between creative fiction and credible fact.[18] In examining the 'realism' of the series though, I do not suggest that the show's narrative is blindly accepted as fact. Aside from very unique cases of young children or primitive cultures witnessing television for the first time, audiences recognise

---

[17] Pinaire, B.K. "Skeptical Opinions: Internet Conspiracies" in *Skeptic*, Vol. 12, No. 1 (2005), p. 26.

[18] For example, see: Knight, P. *Conspiracy Culture: From the Kennedy Assassination to The X-Files*, Routledge, London/New York, 2000, p. 47.

television images as a representation, and do not mistake these images for reality. However, it is contended that the series' claims to authenticity, by being set in a recognisably real world, lend the stories a sense of immediacy which would otherwise be lacking in a surreal or fantasy setting.

Filmic Realism

It is worthwhile to begin examining *The X-Files'* attempts at realism by considering the works of the film theorist, Andre Bazin. It should be noted from the outset that Bazin's discussions of realism were confined almost exclusively to film, rather than television. However, his theories are nonetheless applicable in this context for a number of reasons. Firstly, when we talk of *"The X-Files"* as a text, this necessarily includes the two feature films produced as accompaniments to the television series in 1998 and 2008. More importantly though, the television series itself represents a convergence between the mediums of film and television. Today, it is easy to forget that *The X-Files* was frequently described by critics as 'cinematic' at the time of its broadcast. Likewise, before *The X-Files* ventured into feature films, Chris Carter encouraged comparisons of the TV series with cinema, going so far as to state:

"It looks like a movie; the way it's cut, the way it's directed, the way it's realized, is very theatrical and there's not a lot of stuff on television like it."[19]

As if to illustrate this point, criticism of the first feature film specifically focused on its similarities to the television series. Many reviews argued that *Fight the Future* resembled an elongated episode of the show with a bigger budget. Others claimed that the content of the film was not cinematic enough, too closely resembling the stories presented on the television series. Such criticisms raise questions about the demarcation between film and television texts, a distinction which has been blurred further by the rise of

---

[19] Chris Carter quoted in: Denton, A. "*X-Files:* An Investigation" in *Rolling Stone*, Issue 517 (Yearbook 1995), p. 70.

so-called 'motion picture television,' of which *The X-Files* was a pioneer. If the television series can be described as cinematic, whilst the films themselves can be criticised as too similar to episodic television, why can we not therefore combine theoretical perspectives of both film and television? Ultimately, it is clear that *The X-Files* represents a merging of the styles of film and television and it is for this reason that we will consider the series with reference to the works of film theorists.

Importantly, 'realism' in film and television texts does not simply refer to the plausibility of the narrative, but the formal production practices used to bring the narrative to the screen. Cinematography and sound design are of key importance to convey the events of the story as taking place within a realistic *mise-en-scene*. Equally important is editing; each shot and scene within the narrative is required to maintain a sense of continuity for the audience. As we shall see, in all but a few episodes which pursue unusual formal experiments, *The X-Files* employs these standard Hollywood practices to disguise its status as a fictional text. As with most primetime dramas, continuity editing is used within the series – shots are edited together to maintain spatial and temporal continuity, contributing to the coherence of the narrative.

For Bazin, cinema's realism is a direct result of its photographic nature. Crucially in this regard, *The X-Files* television series was shot on celluloid ("X-Cops" is a notable exception, using digital video). Shooting on 35 mm film is an important feature of the series that distinguishes it from other television texts. By shooting on celluloid, *The X-Files* adheres to the conventions of realism common to most viewers. Viewers may reject alternative filming methods with which they are unfamiliar, as the initial reaction to Peter Jackson's decision to use High Frame Rate (HFR) photography on *The Hobbit* movies demonstrated. Unlike conventional cinema releases, which are shot at 24 frames per second, *The Hobbit* was shot and exhibited at 48 frames per second using HFR technology in 2012. Although this technology is arguably much closer to the human field of vision, the HFR versions of the films were widely dismissed as 'non-cinematic' and resembling a 'video game' upon release. Accordingly, while some may debate the question of which medium can more accurately represent reality, the response to alternative exhibition formats shows that the question is largely irrelevant. For the vast majority of viewers *The X-Files* resembles the celluloid 'reality' that audiences have been indoctrinated to recognise by standard Hollywood production practices.

Another feature common to realist texts is the use of location shooting. Bazin identified film's advantage of being able to shoot on location, rather than being restricted to fixed sets like the theatre. In this context, it is worthwhile noting that *The X-Files*, particularly in its earlier years, relied heavily on the atmosphere generated by its locations. The first five seasons of the series were remarkable for transplanting the Canadian vistas of its Vancouver production base to anywhere in the United States, and beyond. Whilst location shooting is no doubt crucial to the sense of realism generated by a text, *The X-Files* arguably went beyond this by utilizing locations which *substituted* for any number of real-life landmarks. Whether using a British Columbian University to represent FBI headquarters ("Fallen Angel"), or Chinatown to substitute for Hong Kong ("Piper Maru"), *The X-Files* demonstrated Vancouver's remarkable ability to realistically fill in for any number of locations. Numerous commentators have highlighted the prevalence of Vancouver's "generic" and "anonymous" landscapes.[20] For while the exteriors in the show may be instantly recognisable to Vancouverites as landmarks like Stanley Park or Grouse Mountain, to most American and international audiences Vancouver appears unknown, yet somehow relatable. In this way, the series demonstrates Bazin's theories of cinematic realism by emphasising location shooting.

---

[20] For example, see: Brooker, W. "Everywhere and nowhere: Vancouver, fan pilgrimage and the urban imaginary" in *International Journal of Cultural Studies*, Vol. 10, No. 4 (2007), pp. 423-444 and Wolcott, J. "'X' Factor" in *The New Yorker*, Vol. 70, Iss. 9 (April 18 1994), pp. 98-99.

Of course, it could be argued that the use of a *Canadian* city to represent locations within the *United States* negates the series' claims toward realism. Indeed, the favourable Canadian exchange rate was initially an attractive financial incentive for the series to shoot in Vancouver, with generous subsidies making the cost of production significantly cheaper than Los Angeles. But while Vancouver's exchange rate and tax incentives may have helped the show's bottom-line, the real utility of Vancouver as a shooting location derived from that city's ability to artificially mimic almost any other locality. This became even more apparent during the series' later seasons, which were shot in Los Angeles. While Vancouver had substituted for locations as diverse as Washington D.C., Kazakhstan and the Arctic Circle, after filming moved to Los Angeles the series struggled to convincingly replicate such varied locales. In a tacit admission of this, episodes were increasingly set in the south-western United States in later years of the show (in season seven, almost half the season's episodes were set in California where the show was filmed). While the Los Angeles-produced episodes arguably suffered from an inability to convincingly portray locations outside southern California, the show did continue to make heavy use of location shooting in order to represent reality without strictly recreating it. Bazin himself understood the importance of representation over accuracy, arguing that it was only through "artifice" that realism in art could be achieved at all.

The Politics of Realism
Marxist theorists like Louis Althusser argue that the medium of television perpetuates hegemonic ideologies. According to Althusser, the style of dramatic realism employed overwhelmingly in narrative film and television serves only to convey dominant, capitalist structures. Realism serves only to lull audiences into a misguided belief that they are beyond influence, while surreptitiously reaffirming the status quo. Therefore, according to Marxist theorists, realist texts can never be subversive or revolutionary as they merely reiterate bourgeois ideologies.

In contrast, *The X Files* is an example of a realist text that presents a compellingly provocative political ideology. The mythology episodes' explicit attacks on government, combined with the stand-alone episodes' challenges to scientific and institutional authority in the Gothic horror tradition, betray an ideology that undermines the established order. In this way, it can be argued that *The X Files'* foregrounding of its status as a contemporary text that takes place in the same world as its audience, has the effect of *intensifying* its own politically subversive ideology.

The program's strikingly realistic *mise-en-scene* places the narrative events clearly within the lived reality of the audience. In *The X-Files*, costuming, set design, casting, practical effects and particularly locating shooting attest to the series' adherence to the 'realistic mode.' Verisimilitude in the series is achieved through the conscious use of contemporary visual details that audiences instantly recognise. While some computer technology, motor vehicles or cell phones that appear in the show may now seem dated, what is remarkable is how the series has managed to maintain currency more than 20 years after it first aired through the judicious use of these modern visual details. An early example from 1993 is "Ghost in the Machine," where an artificially intelligent operating system hacks into Scully's field reports through her modem connection. Despite the fact that internet penetration in the early 1990s was extremely limited, the series nonetheless used the internet as a plot point or story device in numerous episodes.

But these visual and scenic details are not confined to the show's incorporation of technology to distinguish the events as taking place in the present day. *The X-Files* also uses visual details and other intertextual references to allude to the fact that the program itself takes place in the real world. An example of such visual details can be found in the series' representation of FBI headquarters in Washington D.C. Throughout the series, the office of the agents' superior, Assistant Director Skinner, is shown containing portraits of then real-life U.S. political leaders. President Bill Clinton and

Attorney General Janet Reno are depicted in photographs which hang on the wall of the Assistant Director's office – a strong visual signifier not only of verisimilitude, but also an opportunity for overt political comment from the show. Frequently during the earlier seasons of the show, shots would be framed with Skinner reprimanding the two agents in the foreground while portraits of the President and Attorney General watched on in the background. Whilst the incorporation of these visual details is further evidence of the series' politically subversive character, just as importantly it serves as a prompt to the viewer that the events of the series are occurring in the real world. Details such as these ensure that the viewer cannot simply dismiss *The X-Files* as fantasy because, in the words of Executive Producer John Shiban, the series attempts to, "cast these characters against the real world, or an imagined version of the real world."[21]

Formal Experiments
We can also identify *The X-Files* as a realist text precisely because the series' occasional departures from its set tone, the stylistic flourishes which became more frequent as the show aged and its formula became more familiar, are notable for specifically drawing attention to the series' construction as a television text.

These entries challenge viewers' understanding of the series by incorporating stylistic and narrative choices not common in American television texts. Examples of such episodes include the third season's "Jose Chung's *From Outer Space*," a post-modern use of the unreliable narrator in which the audience is explicitly reminded by a character's dialogue that truth, like reality, is subjective. The sixth season's "Triangle" is another stylised episode, incorporating split-screens, heavy editing and long-takes reminiscent of Hitchcock's *Rope,* in a significant departure from the show's realist style.

---

[21] This quote is transcribed from the "Threads of the Mythology" special feature on the fourth volume of the "mythology" DVD release: *The X-Files Mythology: Super Soldiers*, Region 1, Disc 4, Twentieth Century Fox Home Entertainment, 2005, DVD.

These episodes have been cited as instances where *The X-Files* rejects realism by foregrounding its mediated nature to the viewer. But while it is certainly true that such episodes draw the viewer's attention to the series' status as a fictional construct, within the context of the series' 202 episodes and two feature films, they are extremely limited. In fact, examples of such episodes are noteworthy only *because* they are so rare. Particularly in the early seasons, when *The X-Files* was still establishing its audience, such episodes were non-existent or extremely uncommon. These experimental episodes were probably most common at the height of the series' popularity, when viewers had become familiar with the conventions of the show and the series sought to keep the formula 'fresh.'

An example from the fifth season, "The Post-Modern Prometheus," perfectly demonstrates the degree to which these overtly stylised entries depart from the series' established formula. Unlike other episodes, this one actively draws the viewers' attention to the fact that they are watching a fantasy narrative. The first shot shows a comic book titled 'The Great Mutato' opening, before dissolving into live-action which has been self-consciously filmed in black-and-white (signalling to viewers that this is a mediated representation). As the story unfolds Mulder and Scully track a variant of Mary Shelley's *Frankenstein* monster, a grossly disfigured, Cher-obsessed creature who has been impregnating women by drugging them and breaking into their houses. We learn that this mythical monster has been immortalised as 'The Great Mutato' in a comic book by one of the townspeople, Izzy Berkowitz. In the end, Mulder and Scully find and protect the monster from an angry mob. Ultimately, despite his heartfelt pleas to the townspeople, the monster is captured and sent away in a police car to be punished for his crimes. This prompts Mulder to declare that this is not how the Frankenstein story is "supposed" to end. He argues that the monster in the story is eventually set free to search for his bride and states that he wants to speak to the "writer," just as Izzy enters the room. At this point, a comic book ending ensues where Mulder, Scully, the townspeople and the monster all travel to a concert where the monster finally finds his bride – Cher. The conclusion of the episode is again book-ended by a winking nod to the story's fantastic nature, as we are shown a person's hand turning the pages of a comic book bearing the words, 'Executive Producer: Chris Carter.' By consciously disrupting the closing credits and equating the events of the preceding narrative with a comic, "The Post-Modern Prometheus" again signals its unreality.[22]

There can be no doubt that this episode provides an example of the series rejecting realist conventions. Yet despite the inordinate amount of scholarly attention paid to such episodes (as an instance of *The X-Files'* tendency to break the fourth wall and knowingly wink at the audience) "The Post-Modern Prometheus" represents only a *single* episode within the context of the entire series. Apart from such limited examples, the production overwhelmingly employed standard realist filmmaking techniques. In fact, in later seasons, the show's producers consciously sought to limit the number of these experimental episodes. This may be seen as an acknowledgement of the fact that, ultimately, the audience derives enjoyment from these stylistic flourishes because of their awareness that the series is undermining its usual (realist) formula. On the whole therefore, it can be compellingly argued that *The X-Files* adopts a realist mode to present its stories, including a lifelike *mise-en-scene*, naturalistic acting and unobtrusive editing.

Realism and the Gothic
Whilst "The Post-Modern Prometheus" may stylistically depart from the series' established conventions, it does explicitly continue *The X-Files'* association with the Gothic. Just as the Gothic novels were politically subversive for challenging dominant societal institutions, it has been suggested that Gothic authors such as Mary Shelley also called into question people's own conception of

---

[22] For an excellent summary, see: Jones, C. "'Post-Modern Prometheus,' Postmodern Voices: *The X-Files* and Subjective Storytelling" in *The X-Files and Literature: Unweaving the Story, Unraveling the Lie to Find the Truth* (Ed. Sharon R. Yang), Cambridge Scholars Publishing, Newcastle, 2007, pp. 174-193.

reality. In *Frankenstein*, Dr Victor Frankenstein's attempts to create a living being out of inanimate organs result in a hideous creature that, while animate, resembles nothing of the carefully selected features that comprise its form. Shelley's novel demonstrates mankind's folly in attempting to exercise control over the chaos that is inherent in the natural world. As much as we may like to think otherwise, natural forces are beyond human control.

In a modern context, *The X-Files* serves a similar purpose by constantly making claims to verisimilitude and authenticity in an effort to persuade the audience that the episodes could take place in reality. By using realist narrative techniques and aesthetics, the series meditates on the elusive nature of truth and the existence of 'reality' as we know it.

For example, in the fifth season episode, "Bad Blood," the agents investigate the bloodletting of a victim in North Dakota. The episode's central theme of vampirism can immediately be seen as a connection to the Gothic genre. The story opens with a teenager, Ronnie Strickland, being chased through the woods before a stake is viciously driven through his heart by an unseen pursuer. The next shot reveals that Mulder is the person responsible for impaling the young man, apparently believing Ronnie to be a vampire. When the agents are called to account for Ronnie's death, Mulder and Scully present their own versions of what happened (à la *Rashomon*). Their accounts differ in a number of ways – according to Scully, the town Sheriff was dashing and handsome, whereas in Mulder's version he comes across as a hillbilly with oversized buckteeth. Though such differences of opinion may be expected, occasionally, the protagonists' recollections of events differ wildly. Scully recalls firing at Ronnie and missing before he ran off. However in Mulder's account, Scully's shots directly struck Ronnie in the chest with no effect, before he leapt into the air and fled. "Bad Blood" employs these differing perspectives to comic effect, but the episode can just as easily be read as a commentary on the subjectivity of 'truth.'

Both Mulder and Scully's accounts are presented to the audience within the same realistic *mise-en-scene*. In this way, the series challenges the audience's perceptions of the truth. Though Mulder and Scully's recollection of events are inconsistent, the episode does not favour one account over the other. 'Truth' is shown to be subjective, and open to interpretation. Even the episode's pre-credits sequence (which is apparently an impartial depiction of the events) contains misdirections. The cloaked individual pursuing Ronnie is initially obscured, and only later is it revealed as Mulder (his 'cloak' is actually his trademark trench coat). After impaling Ronnie, Mulder points to the boy's vampire fangs as justification for his actions. The 'fangs' are then revealed to be plastic when Scully removes them. Even, Ronnie's 'death' is eventually shown to be false, as he awakens in the morgue unharmed later in the episode. Therefore we see that just like the Gothic novels of Shelley and Bram Stoker (the latter of which is specifically referenced in "Bad Blood"), *The X-Files* invites viewers to interrogate their own reality by questioning whether it is even possible to know the truth.

The Impact of Realism
On television, the presentation of characters in a realistic mode encourages viewer identification by implying that the events depicted on-screen might be true. While the audience is no doubt aware that *The X-Files* is a fictional drama series, the use of realist production techniques lends a sense of credibility to the narrative. This suggests that viewers could believe, at some level, that the events of *The X-Files'* narrative could correspond with their own real-world society. The implications for this are clear in a post-9/11 world – for if the fictional events of the series can be taken as even slightly realistic, then *The X-Files'* politically subversive stories of government conspiracy take on far greater potency.

But the audience's identification of the series with reality is not simply theoretical. In practical ways, *The X-Files* actively encourages viewers to believe that the program depicts 'real-life' events.

It is telling to note that the pilot episode, begins with a title-card reading:

THE FOLLOWING STORY IS INSPIRED BY ACTUAL

DOCUMENTED ACCOUNTS

Although this is the only occasion where the series makes such bold claims to authenticity within the text, it is significant that this intertitle appears at the beginning of the first episode and, by extension, the entire series. In claiming to be 'inspired' by real-life events, the series seeks to establish an air of credibility. Likewise, in citing 'documented accounts,' *The X-Files* mimics the form of documentaries.

Another way in which the series echoes documentaries is its use of captions to indicate when and where the story takes place. While this technique became an endlessly parodied staple of *The X-Files*, commentators have noted that this feature lends the stories legitimacy, making the series appear somehow more realistic than other fictional drama series.

This is further reflected in the discourse surrounding *The X-Files*, which at the time of its broadcast focused on the plausibility of the series' storylines. Some journalists even went to the extent of studying phenomena featured on the show as research for their stories. To this day, it is still common for news articles about real-life strange events to namedrop the show. Likewise, officially sanctioned books (including one authored by the series' own science advisor) devoted pages and pages to explaining how the series' storylines were based in fact.[23] Meanwhile, Carter frequently stated in interviews that the writers' story ideas came from real-life events, stating, "I'm constantly reading magazines and

---

[23] Numerous official and unofficial publications have sought to emphasise the series' basis in reality, including: Goldman J. *The X-Files: Book of the Unexplained* (Vol. 1 and 2), Simon & Schuster, London, 1995/1996; Simon, A. *The Real Science of The X-Files: Microbes, Meteorites, and Mutants,* Touchstone, New York, 2001; White, M. *The Science of The X-Files,* Legend Books, London, 1996.

newspapers. I pick up all the things you'd think of: *Science, Discovery, Scientific American*, any newspaper with a good science section."[24] Therefore, from the outset the program attempts to lay claims to a degree of legitimacy. This desire to incorporate real-life events into the series manifests itself in numerous episodes, but particularly in the series' complex back-story.

Historical Realism

As we saw in the previous chapter, the suggestion of government misdeeds in *The X-Files* is commonplace and these storylines are evidence of the program's politically subversive nature. However, the series goes further than simply implicating the U.S. government in imagined, fantastic conspiracies (which would possibly serve to keep the series' paranoid and subversive politics at arm's length for the viewer). Instead, the show actively seeks to incorporate real-life historical events into its mythology, thereby lending the stories a greater sense of authenticity. This incorporation of historical events into the series' backstory affirms *The X-Files'* overall perspective that not only has the government engaged in morally questionable activities in the past, but that the population is being deceived about the 'truth' of history. The influence of historical realism on viewers is clear, with Hollywood's presentations of history greatly impacting on the audience's own understanding of the past.[25]

The X-Files began to employ this technique of melding historical fact with fictional storylines towards the beginning of the third season. In the early third season episode, "Paper Clip," Mulder and Scully learn that as part of the U.S. government's efforts to create a human/alien hybrid, medical data has been collected on innocent civilians, including Mulder's sister and Scully herself. "Paper Clip" incorporates the *real-life* history of the American government's secret effort to extradite Nazi war criminals to the

---

[24] Chris Carter quoted in: Lipsky, D. "Chris Carter in the Virtue of Paranoia" in *Rolling Stone*, Iss. 533 (March 1997), p. 50.
[25] For example, see: Toplin, R. B. *History By Hollywood* (2nd Ed.), University of Illinois Press, Urbana/Chicago, 2009.

U.S. so that their scientific knowledge could be exploited. This intermingling of fact and fiction may serve to confuse the viewer, who is unaware which aspects of the series' storylines are true, and which are invented by the show's writers. The storylines can thus become as real for viewers as their own lived reality. Indeed, some viewers have even commented that they must "remind" themselves of the show's fictional nature.[26]

The series encourages just this response to its storylines not only through the incorporation of real-life events into its fictional mythology, but also through stylistic choices which heighten the degree of verisimilitude for the viewer. For instance, in the fourth season episode, "Musings of a Cigarette Smoking Man," the series suggests that the arch-villain of the show is in fact responsible for the assassination of President Kennedy. Along with this incorporation of a real-life historical event into the narrative, the series' depiction of the assassination itself makes numerous intertextual references to Oliver Stone's *JFK*, ostensibly in an attempt to echo that film's claims of historical accuracy. Moreover, the episode also posits that the Cigarette Smoking Man was responsible for Martin Luther King's assassination. This portion of the episode consciously employs black-and-white cinematography, in order to visually echo the credibility afforded to documentary footage. Once again, in this example we see the series blurring the boundaries between real-life history and entertainment.

The series' creator has publicly acknowledged the Watergate scandal as a formative event, and references to these events are prominent throughout *The X-Files* – for example, in the second season's "Little Green Men," Mulder and Scully meet surreptitiously in the car park of the Watergate hotel after they are reassigned to other duties. Similarly in season six, "One Son" shows Mulder threatening the Cigarette Smoking Man at gunpoint in one of the hotel's dimly lit suites. The use of such recognisable

---

[26] For example, see: Delasara, J. *Poplit, Popcult and The X-Files: A Critical Exploration*, Mcfarland & Company Inc. Publishers, Jefferson, 2000, p. 23.

locations acts as a point of identification for the viewer, heightening the show's claims of authenticity. Admittedly, the show occasionally used fictional localities in its storylines. For example, the events of the pilot, take place in 'Bellefleur, Oregon' (a nonexistent place, named for Chris Carter's hometown of Bellflower, California). But aside from these occasionally fictionalised locales, the show overwhelmingly employs *real-life* landmarks to foreground its verisimilitude, and the events of the narrative very often occur in locations and settings that are recognisable to the audience.

Of course, *The X-Files'* focus on historical conspiracy theories such as the JFK assassination and Watergate is perhaps to be expected of a series that deals so heavily in paranoid imagery. However, the series is equally willing to engage in paranoid revisions of other historical events for dramatic purposes. For instance, the Vietnam War and its veterans feature in multiple stories. The second season episode, "Sleepless," posits that the U.S. government experimented on soldiers to prevent them from sleeping. Likewise, "Unrequited" presents the military as complicit in efforts to cover-up the presence of U.S. soldiers still missing in action. But perhaps the most potent example of the series revising historical fact comes during the fifth season premiere. In "Redux," Mulder listens as a U.S. Department of Defense employee explains how UFOs and aliens are merely propaganda tools for what Eisenhower called America's 'military industrial complex.' In one sequence, the whistleblower explains to Mulder how over the past fifty years innocent civilians have been abducted by their own government to further military research projects, while the public has been fed bogus stories of alien abduction in order to distract from these activities. He further states that America is in the business of "war," and that the populace is kept compliant through fear in order to stimulate economic activity. The sheer volume of information conveyed in this scene is significant. Indeed, the pace with which the dialogue is narrated serves only to confound viewers, unsure about what represents factual history and the series' own revision of history. But the narration itself is not the only technique that this episode employs to blend historical fact with contemporary fiction. Once again recalling a similar scene in *JFK*, real-life footage is played on the screen as the dialogue recounts the 'true' history of the Cold War. The use of historical stock footage in this manner serves to represent the events of the series as taking place within our own lived reality, making the fantastic nature of the episode's storyline seem somehow more accurate.

The series goes even further in the following episode, blurring the distinction between reality and fiction by inserting Mulder and Scully's superior, Skinner, into *present day* footage of congressional hearings on cloning. "Redux II" therefore depicts one of the show's central fictional characters interacting with real-life politicians and powerbrokers. A similar technique is used in "Drive," where *The X-Files* 'interrupts' regular programming to open with a Fox newsflash. The stylistic conventions employed by the program serve to suggest that the series' stories are based partially in fact. Such production choices further add to the discourse, encouraged by the producers, that the events depicted in *The X-Files* take place 'within the realm of extreme possibility.'

Realism in the Age of Terror
The X-Files' first feature film, *Fight the Future*, begins with the bombing of a federal government building in Dallas. For this sequence the filmmakers went to great lengths to ensure that the imagery appeared as authentic as possible, even enlisting real FBI agents to assist with filming.

Tellingly however, the bombing depicted in the film is not the responsibility of terrorists; rather the film suggests that the Syndicate destroyed the building to conceal the bodies of victims of an alien virus. As Mulder's source, Alvin Kurtzweil (Martin Landau), tells him, "they" destroyed the building in order to "hide" something. In this instance, 'they' is of course suggestive of the government, rather than terrorists. Additionally, the film consciously seeks to evoke memories of the last major terrorist attack on U.S. soil before 9/11 – the bombing of the Alfred P. Murrah Federal Building in 1995 in Oklahoma City, which killed 168 people. The destroyed building in the film closely resembles news footage of the Oklahoma City bombing, and this replication of familiar imagery contributes to the audience's sense of unease during this scene. Accordingly, we see an example of the series incorporating real-life imagery in a politically subversive manner by suggesting that authorities themselves, and not terrorists, are responsible for attacks on U.S. citizens.

However, the discourse surrounding the series is not entirely consistent with this approach. Although the series' producers repeatedly drew attention to the supposed 'reality' of the narrative, they nevertheless sought to distance *The X-Files* from attacks that the series stoked anti-government fervour. Understandably nervous about such accusations, Carter defended the series by stressing that the program itself is entirely fictional, stating, "It's fiction, first of all – we make this stuff up."[27] In "Tunguska," the show juxtaposes Mulder and Scully against a right-wing group of domestic terrorists seeking to overthrow the government, ostensibly to highlight the differences between their approaches. Likewise, in "The Pine Bluff Variant" Mulder goes undercover within an ultranationalist terrorist group to prevent the release of a deadly bio-toxin. Upon discovering that the government created and sanctioned the release of the chemical weapon, Mulder remonstrates with a CIA agent. When Mulder threatens to go public with claims that the government knowingly tested bio-toxins on the American population, the CIA agent asks him what such an action would accomplish. His response ridicules Mulder's position, questioning whether his ultimate goal is to topple the U.S. government, and succinctly contrasts Mulder's position with the extremist terrorist cell he has just infiltrated.

---

[27] Chris Carter quoted in: Wild, D. "X-Files: Undercover" in *Rolling Stone*, Issue 524 (July 1996), p. 58.

While it is easy to see why some have accused the show of encouraging such connections by consciously invoking real-life images within its fictional storylines, Carter argues that the examples
cited above make the politics of the show clear to viewers:

*"People have asked me about the connection between The X-Files and the
Oklahoma bombing. And as I've tried to make clear, I'm saying question
the government, not overthrow it. This is not a revolutionary show."*[28]

Later in the life of the series, a bizarre instance occurred where the
writers predicted, with remarkable accuracy, the events of 9/11.
The pilot for *The X-Files'* spin-off series, *The Lone Gunmen*, dealt
with a plot by arms dealers and war profiteers to fly commercial
airliners into the World Trade Centre in New York. Remarkably,
this episode aired on 4 March 2001, only six months before the
events of 9/11. Since then, this storyline has itself become the focus
of paranoid speculation about how a fictional series could have
predicted these events, with conspiracy theorists pinpointing the
episode's claim of U.S. government involvement in the attacks as
evidence of a real-life cover up. The show's writers have understandably taken steps to publicly distance their fictional narrative
from the tragedy that followed. Speaking before the tenth anni-
versary of the attacks, writer Vince Gilligan pointed out that plan-
ning for the attacks began well before the episode's broadcast,
reasoning that, "[The World Trade Centre] seems like a pretty obvious target, hence the fact we thought of it, I suppose."[29] Although *The X-Files* was certainly not responsible for the events of
9/11, this remarkable example of life imitating art is perhaps further proof that the events of 9/11 played a large part in the end of
that series.

---

[28] Chris Carter quoted in: Wild, D. "X-Files: Undercover" in *Rolling Stone*, Issue 524 (July 1996), p. 58.

[29] Vince Gilligan quoted in: Archive of American Television, "Interview – Vince Gilligan," 9 August 2011. Retrieved from: http://www.emmytvlegends.org/interviews/people/vince-gilligan (accessed 23 September 2015).

DENY EVERYTHING
POST-MODERNISM AND *THE X-FILES*

We have already seen that *The X-Files* adopted a politically subversive viewpoint, and that it employed a powerfully realistic style to present this viewpoint. But to assert that the contemporary events of 9/11 could impact on the audience's willingness to engage with the series' fictional storylines, we must first accept that there could be some intersection between *The X-Files'* fiction and real-life fact.

The collision between reality and fantasy is a quintessentially post-modern notion, perhaps as readily identifiable with post-modernism as Marshall McLuhan's 1964 adage: "the medium is the message." One theorist whose own work owes a great debt to McLuhan is Jean Baudrillard, the French philosopher and writer. Baudrillard sees post-modern society as characterised by a process of 'simulation.' He argues that television does not simply reflect or reproduce reality, but rather it has *become* our reality - "a hyperreality" which takes on such a degree of meaning that it supplants our own lived experience.[30] This blurring of boundaries – such as the convergence of the film and television mediums, or the distinction between reality and fiction – is critical to post-modernism.

---

[30] Baudrillard, J. "The Implosion of Meaning in the Media" in *Simulacra and Simulation* (Translated by Sheila Faria Glaser), Ann Arbor, Michigan, University of Michigan Press, 1994, p.81.

This chapter analyses *The X-Files* with reference to Baudrillard's theories of 'simulation' and the 'hyperreal.' We will see that *The X-Files* exemplifies Baudrillard's theories by aggressively confronting the breakdown between reality and fiction. We have already seen how the series' presentation of its supernatural stories within a realistic *mise-en-scene* may call into question viewers' conceptions of their own reality. Specific episodes of the series also engage with issues such as the pervasiveness of technology, while others undertake unusual formal experiments that make explicit claims towards post-modernity. While the show's most famous aphorism may well assure us that the 'truth' can be found somewhere out there, we will see that the series reaffirms a post-modern belief that, on television at least, we can 'Trust No One.'

The Post-Modern Files

There has been considerable scholarly debate devoted to the question of whether or not *The X-Files* is an example of a post-modern text. Some have used the program's preoccupation with 'the truth' to argue that the series strongly rejects post-modernism.[31] After all, *The X-Files'* notion of a singular truth is contrary to the post-modernist idea that truth is ultimately unknowable. In contrast though, other academics have cited the series as a textbook example of post-modernism, arguing that the series' form and content are overwhelmingly post-modern.[32] But how is it possible for commentators to hold such divergent perspectives? Perhaps because *The X-Files* is often simply *assumed* to be post-modern, with no consideration given to the way in which the series challenges accepted definitions of post-modernism. Indeed, the series raises questions about our understanding of post-modernism itself.

---

[31] For example, see: Reeves, J. L., Rodgers, M. C. & Epstein, M. "Rewriting Popularity: The Cult Files" in *Deny All Knowledge: Reading The X-Files* (Ed. David Lavery, Angela Hague and Marla Cartwright), Syracuse University Press, Syracuse, 1996, pp. 22-35.

[32] For example, see: Booker, K. M. "It's the Libidinal Economy, Stupid: *The X-Files* and the Politics of Postmodern Desire" in *Strange TV: Innovative Television Series from* The Twilight Zone *to* The X-Files," Greenwood Press, Westport CT, 2002, pp. 121-149; and Kellner, D. "*The X-Files* and the Aesthetics and Politics of Postmodern Pop" in *The Journal of Aesthetics and Art Criticism*, Vol. 57, No. 2 (Spring 1999), pp. 161-175.

The Hyperreal

In a world characterised by simulation, or hyperreality, Baudrillard considers that television is perhaps the ultimate simulator because we take its presence for granted. He writes that TV "watches," "alienates," "manipulates" and "informs" us, but simultaneously the audience must depend on an external perspective of events, an analysis that is not their own, to form their conception of reality.[33] *The X-Files* has interrogated this question of television and technology as manipulative 'simulators' on numerous occasions.

Season seven's "First Person Shooter" depicts a video game where the players are killed by the uncompromising realism of the virtual experience. Similarly, "Kill Switch" presents a world in which people are able to upload their entire consciousness, their existence, onto the internet. More than any other entry however, "Wetwired" shows the series' ability to actively engage with Baudrillard's theories. As described in the previous chapter, this episode depicts a television signal which is able to subliminally influence the mind of the viewer, causing the audience to experience paranoid hallucinations indistinguishable from reality and eventually driving them to kill. After witnessing a Bosnian war criminal on the nightly news, a viewer begins to see the war criminal's face in his neighbours, the police, and even his own wife. Agent Mulder explains that the television signal amplified the perpetrator's anxieties into a form of "dementia," with the viewer's most elemental fears played out in a kind of "virtual reality." In this way, *The X-Files* explicitly demonstrates how television audiences may be unable to distinguish between their own lived reality and the events portrayed on the television screen. The similarities between the narrative of "Wetwired," and Baudrillard's own description of television as a presence that "alienates" and "manipulates" its viewers, are immediately apparent.

---

[33] Baudrillard, J. "The end of the panopticon" in *Postmodern After-Images: A Reader in Film, Television and Video* (Ed. Peter Brooker and Will Brooker), Arnold, London, 1997, p. 164.

Baudrillard's view of television has been described as a form of "covert attack," wherein reality is gradually supplanted by an artificial illusion, or "electronic mirage."[34] This insidious description of television echoes *The X-Files'* own depiction of viewers who are so completely subsumed by the medium that they lose all control over their impulses. Significantly, as in many of the show's storylines, the government is revealed as the party responsible for the offending television signal in "Wetwired." During the episode Mulder challenges his mysterious government source, X (Steven Williams), about whether the signal could be used to influence voting and purchasing decisions. In response, X scornfully asks Mulder if he thinks "they" would stop at only manipulating commerce and politics. In this way, the informant's ominous response reiterates Baudrillard's characterisation of television as an 'attack.' *The X-Files* clearly presents a sinister view of television as a form of control over the audience.

Importantly however, "Wetwired" is not simply a restatement of the postmodernist theories of writers such as Baudrillard or McLuhan. Whilst television is ultimately shown to be responsible for the murderous acts of the individuals in the episode, it is important to remember the medium through which this cautionary tale is delivered: a commercial television series. "Wetwired" therefore also serves as a satirical jab at those who claim that television viewing habits influence people towards violent behaviour. For example, during the episode Mulder ridicules the notion that television viewers are simply "empty vessels" who consume every piece of information that is "fed" to them before acting on it. With this dialogue, the show explicitly undermines the influence of television, arguing that the audience is sophisticated enough to distinguish between their own reality and the mediated representation of television. Therefore whilst Baudrillardian theories are clearly demonstrated in this episode, it is unclear whether *The X-Files* supports or subverts these theories.

---

[34] Sconce, J. *Haunted Media: Electronic Presence from Telegraphy to Television*, Duke University Press, Durham/London, 2000, p. 169.

The 'Old' and 'New' Mediums

The X-Files is equally ambiguous when it comes to a distinction that is integral to Baudrillard's theories – the boundary between cinema and television. As we have seen in our examination of the series' realism, by employing cinematic techniques and filming styles *The X-Files* clearly blurs the boundaries between film and television. This is in stark contrast to Baudrillard, who observes a strict distinction between the fascination and seduction of the cinema, and the negative aspects of television's 'new' medium.

As a television series, *The X-Files* is ostensibly an example of the 'new' medium. However it must not be forgotten that the text is also a film series with two feature films, *Fight the Future* and *I Want to Believe*, having been released under the ambit of *The X-Files*. Baudrillard argues that a straightforward distinction exists between television and cinema – for him, the cinematic medium is always able to maintain a distance between the image and the spectator, while television fuses the image and reality to become 'the hyperreal.'[35] But this apparently straightforward distinction cannot be sustained with reference to *The X-Files*. Whilst Baudrillard may consider television obscene because of its immediacy, we can only wonder what he would make of *The X-Files*, a television series that segued into a film, *Fight the Future*, which was continued by the television series and another film, *I Want to Believe*, only to be revisited in 2016 with another episodic television series.

Many critics and commentators have noted the degree to which *The X-Files* straddles the boundaries between film and television. Indeed, there appears to be no clear demarcation between the films and the television series, which is frequently referred to as 'cinematic.' The producers themselves have encouraged associations of the television series with film. Frequently, those involved with the show would compare individual episodes of the television series to films. While such comparisons may partly be

---

[35] For a detailed discussion, see: Constable, C. "Jean Baudrillard" in *Film, Theory and Philosophy* (Ed. Felicity Coleman), Acumen, Durham, 2009, pp.212-221.

ɪᴍᴏᴛɪᴠated by the series' narrative content and production, the similarities with film are also used as an implicit sign of the show's quality. Speaking of the two- and three-part episodes which were common to *The X-Files*, Chris Carter once stated:

"We were doing shows that were verging on feature length, stories that were worthy of a more grand-scale execution. And we kept hearing, 'This is better than most movies you see in the theatre.'"[36]

Paradoxically however, the film incarnations have been criticised for being too similar to the television series. One reviewer described the 1998 feature film as an "unexceptional episode" which took place on the big screen, arguing that the storyline was derived from the television show's "often superior" instalments.[37] Similarly, in 2008, the second feature film was criticised for its languid pacing, with some critics commenting that the storyline was scarcely sufficient to sustain an entire episode of the television series. Therefore, we can see that commentators cite the television series' similarities with film, while film critics simultaneously attack the films' perceived similarities to television. Although this blurring of boundaries is arguably further evidence of the show's post-modernism, it is problematic when considering the show in relation to Baudrillard's theories. The apparently straightforward distinction that Baudrillard argues exists between cinema and television irrevocably breaks down when applied to *The X-Files*.

"The medium is the message"
While it may be difficult to reconcile the 'cinematic' look and feel of *The X-Files* television series with Baudrillard's views, the show perfectly encapsulates many of his other ideas in relation to television's dilution of reality. As we have already seen, when analysing *The X-Files* commentators tend to focus on the show's

---

[36] Chris Carter quoted in: Duncan, J. *The Making of The X-Files: Fight the Future*, HarperPrism, New York, 1998, p. 5.
[37] Vitaris, P. "*The X-Files: Fight the Future* (Review)" in *Cinefantastique*, Vol. 30, No. 7/8 (October 1998), p. 51.

unusual formal experiments, the post-modern episodes of the series which depart from the show's usual realist style. Such episodes are notable for jettisoning the show's predominantly realist style. The rarity of these formal experiments serves to confirm that the series overwhelmingly used realism to allow viewers to identify with the narrative onscreen.

By contrast, the series' post-modern episodes use exaggerated performances, unorthodox camera angles and often surreal scenarios to draw the viewer's attention to the fact that they are witnessing a mediated representation of reality. The previous chapter looked at the example of "The Post-Modern Prometheus" as evidence of the series' connections with the Gothic horror tradition and the relative scarcity of these formal experiments within the canon of the series. Notably though, the self-awareness with which this episode approaches its subject would likely have drawn approval from Baudrillard. The story takes Mulder and Scully to a small town where the townsfolk are terrorised by a modern-day monster, whilst being preoccupied with the fact that these experiences could see them appear on the (real-life) *Jerry Springer Show*. Drawing attention to the absurdity of this situation, Scully remarks to Mulder that they are witnessing a culture for whom tabloid media has become a standard that people use to assess their own existence or, in other words, it has become their "reality." Scully argues that the townspeople are symptomatic of a culture that is "obsessed" by the media, one that judges success or failure solely by whether their story is able to capture the attention of a daytime talk show.

This sentiment supports the notion that the media (particularly television media) has come to define reality for its audience. It is equally important that Scully's commentary on the media occurs in a fictional television series, serving to illustrate Baudrillard's point that the medium of television has itself become reality. Indeed, consider whether or not Scully is referring to the fictional media of the story? Or is she referring to the real-life media, of which the fictional series is itself apart? In this example, *The X-Files* depicts a *fictional* television character commenting on the *real-life* influence of the medium, whilst appearing in an episode that self-consciously draws the viewer's attention to the fact that they are watching a television show. Discerning 'reality' in this example becomes so fraught, that the audience is reminded of Baudrillard's assertion that the medium of television filters everything; dissolving "TV into life," and "life into TV."[38]

By signalling its own status as a mediated representation, "The Post-Modern Prometheus" is an extreme example of *The X-Files'* formal experiments. However another stylised episode from season seven provides an example of *The X-Files* attempting to conceal its fictional nature. In "X-Cops," the series intentionally blurs the distinction between reality and fiction as Mulder and Scully appear within an episode of a real-life television series. The episode's writer, Vince Gilligan, has indicated that he believes the premise of *Cops* (portraying the exploits of real-life police and criminals as entertainment for television) is uniquely American. Accordingly, "X-Cops" is presented not as an episode of *The X-Files*, but as an entry in the popular reality series. According to Supervising Producer Paul Rabwin, the writer had intended for the episode not to feature an opening titles sequence or anything else that could identify it as an episode of *The X-Files*. Gilligan had originally hoped that this would be an instalment of *Cops* that "just happened" to feature Mulder and Scully.[39] The photography of the show actively seeks to emulate the *verite* style of *Cops* in both look and feel, shooting on high-definition video for the first and only time, in a departure from the series' traditional use of 35mm film (which Baudrillard considers crucial to maintaining distance between the medium and the spectator).[40] The episode

---

[38] Baudrillard, J. "Precession of Simulacra" (translated by Paul Foss and Paul Patton) in *Art/Text*, No. 11 (Spring 1983), p. 34.

[39] Paul Rabwin quoted in: Shapiro, P. *all things: The Official Guide to The X-Files Vol. 6*, HarperCollins Publishers, New York, 2001, p.153.

[40] For an excellent summary, see: Bosley, R.K. "Dark Matters" in *American Cinematographer*, Vol. 89, No. 8 (August 2008), pp. 26-37.

was shot in Venice, Los Angeles, giving a gritty, urban feel to the proceedings. By shooting their actors hand-held, with limited edits in the style of a well-known reality TV show, *The X-Files'* producers made claims to realism and blurred the distinction between the fictional events depicted in the series, and those of real-life. For instance, the episode's director argued that "X-Cops" emphasised the "realism" and "naturalness" of the events it depicted.[41]

According to Baudrillard though, *nothing* about "X-Cops" could be described as 'real' or 'natural.' Conversely, "X-Cops" demonstrates the potential for television to simulate our world through artificial images that resemble reality – in this case, the perceived 'reality' of a seedy Los Angeles neighbourhood. This scenario leads inexorably to a situation where it is impossible to distinguish between the simulation and the reality.

Hollywood North

While "X-Cops" is notable for foregrounding its simulation of Los Angeles, perhaps the most compelling evidence of *The X-Files'* post-modern nature comes from the series' original shooting location. Although the stories were set in locations across the United States (and beyond), from 1993 until 1998 *The X-Files* was shot in and around Vancouver, Canada. As previous chapters have noted, the utility of Vancouver as a shooting location was in the city's 'anonymity' and its ability to replicate most other North American locations. In this way, *The X-Files'* use of a *foreign* city to accurately represent America echoes Baudrillard's own theories of the 'hyperreal.' By using a Canadian city to represent American locations, the series arguably draws attention to the falseness of 'reality' itself.

For example, in the second season episode, "Anasazi," the producers faced a dilemma finding a Canadian location to represent New Mexico. One producer explained that while Vancouver was

---

[41] Director Michael Watkins quoted in: Persons, D. "The Making of X-Cops" in *Cinefantastique*, Vol. 32, Iss. 3 (October 2000), p. 29.

able to convincingly duplicate numerous locations within continental North America, "the one thing they didn't have was desert."[42] Accordingly, the production crew's solution was to use an abandoned quarry, literally painting the entire location red in order to resemble the south-western United States. This serves as a dramatic example of the simulation which Baudrillard sees everywhere – with the series' art department constructing a façade to represent a real-life location, which is accepted as fact by the audience – the inevitable result is the eventual destruction of reality itself into the hyperreal.

The final episode of *The X-Files* to be filmed before the move to Los Angeles was perhaps appropriately titled, "The End." In the story, Mulder and Scully investigate an assassination which occurs in Vancouver. This storyline has been acknowledged by the episode's writer, Chris Carter, as a cheat – this scenario could never occur in real-life because, "Canada really isn't within the FBI's jurisdiction."[43] Yet by employing the conventions of realism, and by blurring the boundaries between representation and reality, the series clearly encourages viewers to believe that stories such as this could be true.

However, we can see further evidence of hyperreality in *The X-Files'* use of its locations within the narrative. For instance, in the show Scully's residence is apparently in Annapolis, Maryland, but the exterior shots of her apartment building for the first five seasons were taken from suburban Vancouver. Confusingly, whilst Annapolis exists as a real suburb of Maryland, the character's street address provided on-screen is fictional. Meanwhile, the real-life Vancouver location is used only for establishing and exterior shots, with scenes of the interiors filmed on a studio set. Following the show's move to Los Angeles, a studio back-lot was used as the exterior of Scully's apartment building (even though it scarcely

---

[42] Executive Producer R.W. Goodwin quoted in: Hurwitz, M. & Knowles, C. *The Complete X-Files: Behind the Series, the Myths, and the Movies*, Insight Editions, San Rafael, 2008, p. 68.
[43] Chris Carter quoted in: Meisler, A. *Resist or Serve: The Official Guide to The X-Files Vol. 4*, Harper Collins, New York, 1999, p. 281.

resembled the tree-lined street that had been established earlier in the series). Finally, and despite the exterior of the apartment building dramatically changing appearance after the fifth season, the interior set of Scully's apartment nonetheless remained the same. This example demonstrates the contortions through which 'reality' can become confused with televisual fiction. Ultimately, the result is the destruction of any original referent by which reality itself can be measured.

It has been noted elsewhere that fans travel to the series' Vancouver shooting locations in order to have the experience of visiting sites like 'Scully's apartment.' Although they would likely be familiar with the show's production methods (aware that these shooting locations are only exterior representations of a studio set) these landmarks nevertheless take on an added meaning for fans of the show. In this way, we can see how reception of the text is ultimately shaped by the viewers themselves. [44]

The series even comments on this relationship in its penultimate episode, "Sunshine Days." In this entry, a man is killed while breaking into a property that he believes is the 'Brady Bunch house.' Agent Reyes (Annabeth Gish) later points out that *The Brady Bunch* was actually shot on a soundstage in Hollywood. She notes that the exterior shots of the house where taken at a different location in Studio City, and even claims to have a picture of this location. Through this dialogue, the episode makes it clear that the notion of an original 'Brady Bunch house' is an abstraction – the house was made up of artificial sets and establishing shots, so no 'original' can ever exist. In the narrative, the occupant of the property is a troubled fan who telekinetically recreates *The Brady Bunch* set in his own house in order to feel comfortable. Unable to move on from his favourite television show, he instead recreates the familiar environments with his mind.

---

[44] For an excellent summary, see: Brooker, W. "Everywhere and nowhere: Vancouver, fan pilgrimage and the urban imaginary" in *International Journal of Cultural Studies*, Vol. 10, No. 4 (2007), pp. 423-444.

While the series presents an exaggerated example, it is true that fans of *The X-Files* travel to the show's filming locations as a sort of pilgrimage. Accordingly, fictional events can impact on the series' audience to the extent that viewers will actively seek out locations used within the series. While admittedly only hard-core fans will be dedicated enough to undertake such a journey, this behaviour serves to evidence the illusory distinction between *The X-Files'* fictional stories and real-life events. If the audience's reception of the series can influence their own interpretation of reality, then it is equally possible that real-life events could influence the audience's reception of the text.

EVERYTHING DIES
THE X-FILES AS POP CULTURAL ARTEFACT

Until now, this book has examined in detail the suggestion that because *The X-Files* was ostensibly politically subversive, and because it set its stories within a real world indistinguishable from their own, post-9/11 audiences would be reluctant to engage with a text synonymous with conspiracy and government misdeeds. This contention is arguably supported by post-modern reception theory, which emphasises the influence that television texts have over our conception of reality.

Following the premiere of *The X-Files'* final season in November 2001 (a mere two months after the events of 9/11), the show's ratings fell dramatically and never again reached the heights that they had previously. It is contended that these ratings were the result of a viewer backlash – following the traumatic events of 9/11, patriotism surged as Americans looked to their government for leadership. Faith in the U.S. President skyrocketed to levels rarely seen before or since. In this environment, it is easy to understand how *The X-Files*, a series which at its core suggested that the U.S. government was a flawed and corrupted institution, could fall out of favour. However, it is supremely difficult to attribute the series' end to any one reason. The series' ratings had been in decline well before Mulder's character was written out of the show, before 9/11 and even before the series' mythology was purportedly resolved. While this suggests that the drop in ratings before season nine was merely part of an ongoing trend, the fact remains that viewer numbers declined gradually over time before the final season, and only *after* 9/11 did the ratings suddenly and dramatically fall. However, just because the series' popularity waned after 9/11, this does not definitively establish that the American public's attitude had shifted because of that event.[45]

Therefore, it is necessary to examine the popular reception of *The X-Files* in detail to determine what other explanations exist for the series' decline. Television ratings are of course one way of gauging television texts' popularity, but they provide only limited demographic information about who has watched programs, with no explanation of *why* viewers watched a certain program (or, in this case, why viewers stopped watching a program). Accordingly, this chapter will attempt to shed some light on the tastes of *The X-Files'* audience.

Television texts do not exist within a vacuum. Whilst 9/11 provides a compelling cultural explanation for the series' decline in popularity, it is not the only explanation. Producers of *The X-Files* have expressly cited changes in U.S. society after 9/11 as a reason for the series' decline in popularity, but this assertion cannot be blindly accepted without taking into account the ways in which the show itself changed during the course of its broadcast run. Some believe that attributing the end of *The X-Files* solely to the events of 9/11 places too much importance on cultural factors, ignoring the obvious changes to the show's style and content which took place at the same time. If this is indeed the case, I will briefly examine other factors that have been cited for *The X-Files'* abrupt cessation.

---

[45] For detailed analyses of the final season's reception, see: Brown, S. "Memento Mori: The Slow Death of *The X-Files*" in *Science Fiction Film & Television*, Vol. 6, Issue 1 (2013), pp. 7-22; and Cantor, P.A. "The Truth Is Still Out There: *The X-Files* and 9/11" in *Homer Simpson Marches on Washington – Dissent through American Popular Culture* (Ed. Timothy M. Dale and Joseph J. Foy), The University Press of Kentucky, Lexington, 2010, pp. 75-96.

Longevity in Popular Television Texts
Many commentators have drawn attention to the extraordinary lifespan of *The X-Files*, with a consensus emerging that nine seasons is an unusually long time for a television series to remain on-air, much less maintain significant popularity. Indeed, academics have argued that the numerous representations of immortality in later seasons as a pathetic and pitiful condition, in episodes like "Tithonus" and "The Gift," confirm that the writers themselves were aware that their show had lasted too long.[46] Certainly as its broadcast run continued, *The X-Files'* production costs escalated from an early budget of US$1.1 million per episode, to around US$4 million per episode by the final season. Such a massive investment obviously demanded good returns.

Unfortunately though, commercial television texts are generally believed to enjoy only a brief period of popularity before eventually becoming too unprofitable to justify their production. Most commentators maintain that a television series has a limited opportunity where the zeitgeist affords popularity, but that the spirit of the times eventually changes (along with the audience's reception of the text). The discourse surrounding *The X-Files* at the height of its popularity certainly reflects this conventional wisdom, with few predicting that the series would eventually continue into the new millennium.

Significantly, at the time of *The X-Files'* debut *Entertainment Weekly* infamously declared, "We know – this show's a goner."[47] That same show would go on to air for nine seasons, receive dozens of awards and become a pop-cultural phenomenon. One of the plethora of unofficial books published to capitalise on the series' success in 1996, stated that it was "extremely unlikely" that the

---

[46] For example, see: VanWinkle, M. "Tennyson's 'Tithonus' and the Exhaustion of Survival in *The X-Files*" in *The X-Files and Literature: Unweaving the Story, Unraveling the Lie to Find the Truth* (Ed. Sharon R. Yang), Cambridge Scholars Publishing, Newcastle, 2007, pp. 298-311.
[47] Lowry, B. *The Truth Is Out There: The Official Guide to The X-Files* (Vol. 1), HarperCollins Publishers, London, 1995, p. 21.

series would continue past 1998.[48] In the same year, other commentators wrote of the possibility that the series would continue much longer with disbelief. These writers argued that the series had already reached the height of its popularity by the third season, when in fact the zenith of the show's popularity would not come until two years later (measured in terms of average viewer numbers). Meanwhile, during the seventh season of the show, numerous commentators erroneously referred to that year as the "last" season of *The X-Files*, all but ruling out the possibility of a season eight.[49] Even David Duchovny, who famously resisted attempts to continue the show, stated at the time of its broadcast that seven seasons was "enough."

These examples are illustrative of the conventional wisdom in television that a series enjoys only a brief run of popularity. The implication is that *The X-Files* had already fulfilled its potential by the 2001-02 season, with the reduced ratings in its final year seen as proof that the series had outstayed its welcome with viewers.

The problem with this assertion is that it is self-fulfilling. Quite obviously commercial television texts will end once their popularity can no longer justify the considerable expense of their production. But the countless examples of pundits incorrectly predicting the series' end-date demonstrate the falsehood that is inherent in accurately guessing at the lifespan of a television series. Numerous series continue to remain popular for many years, even decades, while predictions of their demise continue. The notion that somehow all television texts have a preordained 'expiry date,' after which their popularity will plummet, is therefore clearly wrong. The announcement in 2015 that *The X-Files* will be revived for a limited event series, more than 20 years after its debut, is further proof that some texts continue to resonate within the zeitgeist for decades. If we accept that few could possibly have predicted

---

[48] Bassom, D. *Anderson + Duchovny: An Extraordinary Story*, Hamlyn, London, 1996, p. 74.
[49] For example, see: Delasara, J. *Poplit, Popcult and The X-Files: A Critical Exploration*, Mcfarland & Company Inc. Publishers, Jefferson, 2000, p. 212-213.

The X-Files' remarkable longevity, it follows that there must be a *reason* for the show's decline in popularity in the 2001-02 season, beyond simply stating that it 'lasted too long.'

The 'Cultural Moment'

One explanation which is often given as the reason for *The X-Files'* cancellation is that the series' 'cultural moment' had passed. The problem is trying to identify, in hindsight, when exactly the series' cultural moment existed. *The X-Files* is frequently mentioned in terms of pre-millennial anxieties, with *The New Yorker* expressly arguing during its broadcast that the show "reflects the end of the millennium."[50] However, this notion that *The X-Files* is entirely bound to an illusory moment before the turn of the millennium seems tenuous. If this were indeed true, we would expect to see a corresponding drop in the series' ratings after 2000 (the date that most lay people identified with the 'new' millennium). In fact, the series' overall popularity remained steady that year. While ratings for the 1999-2000 season had dipped from the show's peak, the series still maintained much of its viewership. Instead, it seems that the 'cultural moment' which the series outlasted was far more tangible, a specific date that signalled America's vulnerability to extremist terrorism for the audience.

In this way, 9/11 can be characterised as a traumatic and symbolic event demonstrating the fallibility of the West. In contrast to the vaguely defined notion of 'the end of the millennium,' the events of 9/11 were accompanied by such radical political and social changes that a subversive text like *The X-Files* saw its popularity slump almost immediately. It is therefore true that the zeitgeist turned against the series. Remarkably however, on this occasion the date when the zeitgeist changed can be pinpointed exactly – 11 September 2001. Before this event, cynicism and paranoia about government were not just confined to the political fringes, but had effectively become mainstream. In contrast, the series' drop in popularity following 9/11 coincided with fundamental societal

---

[50] Wolcott, J. "'X' Factor" in *The New Yorker*, Vol. 70, Iss. 9 (April 18 1994), p. 98.

changed, including the emergence of a powerful consensus in U.S. politics and strong condemnation of opposition voices. Consequently, *The X-Files'* politically subversive tone failed to reflect the U.S. public's newfound conservatism after 9/11.

The X-Files goes to Hollywood

Of course, there are other reasons that have been offered to explain the demise of the series. Critical reception of *The X-Files* gradually soured as the series progressed, and a view has emerged that the show's quality declined progressively from the fifth season onwards. Indeed, long before 9/11 some argued that the series lost that aspect which had made it so distinctive – the grey, atmospheric look of its Vancouver shooting location.

According to many the unique look which Vancouver lent to *The X-Files* was a key factor in the show's success. The dreary Canadian climate proved a perfect accompaniment to the show's sometimes even drearier storylines. In 1997, *The New Yorker* singled out the series' "expressionistic climate" as a reason for its success, noting that the show's dim lighting, and the ever-present rain and fog imbued the visuals with "free floating dread."[51] The signature 'look' of *The X-Files*, and particularly the Vancouver-shot episodes, is something for which the series has become renowned.

Earlier, the series' propensity to challenge the political status quo and question rationality were singled out as explicitly connecting *The X-Files* with the Gothic horror tradition. The show's dark and foreboding setting arguably represents another such connection. The creepy forests and small towns that frequently served as the setting for the series' stories closely resemble similar settings from the Gothic narratives of Shelley, Stoker and Conan-Doyle. Similarly, others have explicitly connected the series with the Gothic arguing that Mulder and Scully represent a kind of modern-day Holmes and Watson. Just as Sherlock Holmes' investigations were set against the windswept moors of England, for the series' first

---

[51] Wolcott, J. "Too Much Pulp" in *The New Yorker*, Vol. 72, Iss.41 (6 January 1997), p. 76.

five seasons Mulder and Scully had the rain-soaked streets of Vancouver as their setting. Many critics lauded this location as central to *The X-Files'* success, giving it a look and feel which was unable to be found elsewhere.

Of course, we must be mindful that critical opinions are not to be privileged over the opinions of the series' audience. While critical acclaim can be used to assess the reception of a text, it is not to be confused with popularity. Critically lauded programs frequently fail to find an audience, just as popular texts can defy critical scorn.

However, the online popularity of *The X-Files* allows us direct access to the opinions of the series' fanbase, where we see that it was not just critics who celebrated the unique look which Vancouver brought to the series. Some viewers clearly disagreed with the series' move to Los Angeles in order to accommodate the wishes of its star. One fan has been quoted as saying that the series' departure from Vancouver was "the most critical component" of the show's drop in quality. Meanwhile, another long-time fan of the series gushed about the "perfect, creepy, woodsy" feel of Vancouver, arguing that the show was forced to "manufacture" that feeling after the relocation to Los Angeles. [52] Indeed, Carter has himself acknowledged that Los Angeles did not offer the "free atmosphere" that had previously been available in Vancouver. [53]

Importantly though, the change in shooting location was not the only event to accompany the start of the sixth season. In June 1998, weeks after the fifth season ended, the first feature film, *Fight the Future*, was released. The movie continued the mythology storyline, revealing the global dimensions of the Syndicate's conspiracy to pave the way for an alien invasion. The film received mostly favourable critical notices, with reviewers generally

---

[52] Kessenich, T. *Examinations: An Unauthorized Look at Seasons 6-9 of The X-Files*, Trafford, Victoria, 2002, p. 8.

[53] This quote is transcribed from "The Truth About Season 6" special feature on the season six DVD release: *The X-Files: The Complete Sixth Season*, Region 4, Disc 6, Twentieth Century Fox Home Entertainment, 2002, DVD.

agreeing that the film captured the essence of the series (notably despite being shot in Los Angeles). The film's box-office was also respectable – *Fight the Future* had one of the biggest opening weekends of any film in 1998, grossing almost $190 million worldwide (more than three times its reported production cost).

Nevertheless, some fans responded negatively to the film, feeling that *Fight the Future's* blockbuster tone and emphasis on visual effects compromised the feel of the show. Despite such grumblings, it is interesting to note that the series' ratings did not fall dramatically the following year. While *The X-Files'* popularity had waned somewhat from the previous season, it was always going to prove hard to maintain that level of hysteria without the anticipation of a summer blockbuster (and the accompanying marketing budget). The opinions of those fans who feel that the series declined following the release of *Fight the Future* may be attributable to the fact that, by that time, the series had now firmly entered the mainstream and was no longer 'their' show. With the hype that accompanied the film's release in 1998, *The X-Files'* status as a commercial product had become undeniable, even if the series' political perspective remained deeply subversive.

With ratings suggesting that the series remained popular, the hard-core fans who dismiss the program following its move to Los Angeles and the release of *Fight the Future* appear to have been reacting emotionally to the show's unprecedented success. The confinement of this backlash to a relatively small group of embittered fans, along with the fact that the series continued for *four* seasons in Los Angeles, suggests that it was not *The X-Files'* move to California alone which killed the series.

'Will they or won't they?': The Mulder and Scully Relationship
Many critical assessments of *The X-Files* note how central Mulder and Scully's relationship was to the success of the show. The chemistry between the two leads, as well as the producers' insistence that their relationship remain platonic, proved an important selling point for the program as it teased viewers with the

possibility of resolution. Time and again, the series foregrounded the relationship between the two main characters, suggesting the possibility that it could develop into a romantic union. This emphasis owes a large debt to those fans who identified themselves as 'shippers' (derived from 'relationshippers'), who would intricately dissect each of Mulder and Scully's interactions. The series cheekily pandered to this sentiment on numerous occasions, such as in the fourth season episode, "Small Potatoes," showing an impostor who is able to physically transform into Mulder attempting to seduce Scully. This scenario was repeated again in "Dreamland," when Mulder switched bodies with a philandering Man In Black who almost immediately sets about wooing Scully. *Fight the Future*, meanwhile, depicts an interrupted kiss between the pair. The sixth season's "Triangle" used the conceit of an alternate reality to show Mulder kiss 'Scully' – a completely different character from 1939 according to the narrative, although still played by Gillian Anderson. The agents are mistaken for husband and wife in "The Rain King," by a hotelier who insists that they must share a room. Similarly, in "Arcadia," the agents go undercover posing as a married couple to investigate a number of mysterious disappearances from a gated housing estate.

These examples illustrate that the series was self-conscious about the lengths taken to defer consummation of Mulder and Scully's relationship. Simultaneously though, the drawn-out nature of the relationship demonstrates that the show's producers were aware of the conventional wisdom that, for a television series, romantic resolution frequently results in cancellation. In this sense, the series paradoxically relied on viewer interest in the unresolved nature of the relationship, just as the writers fought to keep the relationship from ever being consummated. It is therefore clear that a tension existed between the viewer's desire to see Mulder and Scully end up together, and the producers' belief that viewers would desert the show as soon as this event occurred. The series' creator and showrunner was a particularly vocal opponent of the protagonists having any romantic relationships. In the series pilot, the network mandated that Scully should have a boyfriend in order to make her character more relatable, but Carter fought to remove these scenes from the final episode. As he described later:

"People say, "Will Mulder and Scully ever go to bed?" And I say, "You really don't want them to." Because the minute they do...they will become more interested in themselves than in the things that they need to be doing."[54]

Consequently, the series continually deferred any resolution of the relationship. In the seventh season's "Millennium" (a cross-over between *The X-Files* and Chris Carter's other Fox series), we see Mulder and Scully share a midnight kiss on New Year's Eve 1999. Following the kiss, Mulder expresses surprise that the world "didn't end," in reference not only to millennial predictions of the apocalypse, but also a winking nod to the fact that the characters' relationship had been irrevocably changed. [55]

What is interesting to note about this scene is that the series steadfastly refused to acknowledge *any* change in the characters' relationship. Despite the viewer emphasis placed on Mulder and Scully's first real kiss, the very next week the agents continued to investigate cases as if nothing had changed. With the series failing to depict any ramifications for Mulder and Scully's relationship, the kiss was ultimately inconsequential. Part of this is of course a function of the unusual format of *The X-Files* – as the show straddles the boundaries between the 'serial' and the 'series,' the characters' relationships do not develop in a traditional way. While Mulder and Scully certainly grew closer over the course of the show, their characters remained primarily focused on their investigations. The series therefore seeks to satisfy the viewers' appetite for romantic resolution without ever consummating it.

---

[54] Chris Carter quoted in: Lipsky, D. "Chris Carter in The Virtue of Paranoia" in *Rolling Stone*, Issue 533 (March 1997), p. 111.
[55] For an excellent summary, see: Speidel, S. "The Ending Is Out There" in *The X-Files and Literature: Unweaving the Story, Unraveling the Lie to Find the Truth* (Ed. Sharon R. Yang), Cambridge Scholars Publishing, Newcastle, 2007, pp. 312-345.

By constantly deferring resolution in this manner, *The X-Files* reflects the medium of television itself, where closure cannot ever be final. Individual episodes must offer a hint of resolution, while still remaining open-ended enough for the story to continue again the following week.

We have previously seen how the series exploits inconclusive narratives in its standalone episodes, in a nod to the Gothic tradition of depicting dominant societal institutions, like the FBI, as powerless to protect the populace against dark forces. However this avoidance of resolution also characterises the relationship between the show's characters. For much of the series, the audience was constantly teased about the nature of Mulder and Scully's relationship. This continued even until the season eight revelation of Scully's pregnancy, with only vague and ambiguous references to the child's parentage. Eventually, in the season nine episode, "Trust No 1," the dialogue of a minor character reveals that Mulder and Scully conceived the baby off-screen during season seven. In this way, the series managed to avoid showing any consummation of the protagonist's relationship – a remarkable feat given that the series spent nine seasons teasing viewers, and the producers were well aware of the audience's emphasis on the sexual tension between Mulder and Scully. That this consummation could occur off-screen (and not be addressed until two years later) demonstrates the producers' reluctance to expressly acknowledge any romantic union between the pair. In this sense, quite apart from 9/11, one explanation for *The X-Files'* decline in ratings could be that audiences tired of the series' continuing refusal to acknowledge the romantic attraction between Mulder and Scully that was craved by viewers.

It is possible that through failing to ever overtly depict Mulder and Scully becoming romantically involved, instead using only oblique references, the series' audience simply lost patience. If that were the case, the proximity of the series' final season to 9/11 would appear to simply be coincidental. However, if this is the case, the question becomes: why did so many viewers desert the series in its ninth season when this technique of deferring resolution had been employed since the series' inception? The obvious answer would be that by season nine David Duchovny had *permanently* left the series, meaning audiences were well aware that the relationship would never be resolved. But during the series' eighth season, when David Duchovny was contractually obliged to appear in only half the episodes, the series' share of the audience actually increased from the previous year. Despite the character of Mulder being sidelined in the series' penultimate season, viewers nonetheless continued to tune in. For this reason, the overwhelming focus on Mulder and Scully's relationship has arguably been overstated. While a vocal portion of the show's fanbase, the 'shippers,' apparently prioritised the protagonists' relationship above all else, the views of these individuals are no more valid than those who argued strongly against any relationship between the pair. While the sexual tension between the leads was no doubt part of the series' appeal, it could scarcely account for the huge drop in viewers which occurred post-9/11.

It would appear that series creator Chris Carter was correct when he stated that viewers really don't want Mulder and Scully to settle down. Although the irresolution which characterised Mulder and Scully's relationship undoubtedly proved frustrating for viewers – it was *essential* for the continued survival of the series. Had the series expressly depicted a resolution to the protagonists' relationship, this would have almost certainly impacted negatively on the series' commercial prospects. Indeed, the poor box-office and muted critical reaction to the 2008 film, where Mulder and Scully are shown living together in apparent domestic bliss, would seem to confirm that audiences did not watch *The X-Files* just so that they could see the main characters end up together. Rather, it was the tantalising *possibility* that this relationship would be consummated that contributed to the success of the show.

Lies Within Lies: The Unresolvable Mythology

The relationship between the protagonists was not the only aspect of the series which defied resolution. Just as the narratives of many of the series' episodes refused finality, and just as Mulder and Scully's relationship was never adequately resolved, the overarching mythology of the series also failed to ever conclude satisfactorily. At the commencement of the series the primary motivation for Mulder's quest was the search for his missing sister, Samantha, whom he believed to have been abducted by aliens. As the show progressed the search for Samantha gradually receded into the background, as Mulder and Scully sought to expose the conspiracy to conceal the existence of extraterrestrials from the public, and the mysterious men who orchestrated this cover-up. But *The X-Files* clearly relished ambiguity, and revelations from one season were quickly ignored or dismissed in later seasons.

As an example, the second season two-parter "Colony/End Game" introduced an alien bounty hunter sent to earth to dispatch alien clones using a metallic stiletto. When Scully is taken hostage by this bounty hunter, a woman claiming to be Mulder's sister tells him that the only way to kill the bounty hunter is to pierce the base of his neck. Later, in a tense stand-off, a sniper shoots the bounty hunter from behind, apparently with no effect. Then in the third season's final episode, "Talitha Cumi," Mulder discovers an identical stiletto among his father's possessions. When his informant, X, demands that he hand over the stiletto, Mulder asks if it is, "the only way" that they can be killed. X confirms Mulder's suspicions, stating that a "simple gunshot" is ineffective. While this exchange apparently confirms why the bounty hunter walked away from a gunshot unharmed the season before, in the very next episode it is brought into question. In "Herrenvolk," Mulder kills the alien bounty hunter by using the stiletto to pierce his neck, but moments later he inexplicably revives. In season eight's "Without," aired more than *four years* after, Scully shoots the alien bounty hunter in the neck, killing him instantly. Such inconsistencies and contradictions demonstrate the mythology episodes' tendency to raise more questions than they answered. While explanations were offered, these would frequently be revealed as false in subsequent episodes.

This refusal to resolve the many threads of the complex mythology storyline certainly proved frustrating for many viewers – the perception being that the series was exploiting audience goodwill for an answer that would never come. Indeed, the dense plots and intricate character relationships of the mythology episodes in later seasons arguably rendered them impenetrable for casual audiences. Many viewers clearly anticipated a final resolution to the mythology storyline, hopeful that the many questions posed by the series could indeed be answered. But given that the ultimate length of the series was always uncertain (not only to *The X-Files'* audience but to the writers as well) it is unsurprising that continuing the mythology storyline involved a degree of improvisation with each new season. The creators have since acknowledged that these episodes were not written with any overarching idea of where the story would end up at the series' conclusion. Indeed, in the fourth season episode, "Tunguska," the treacherous Alex Krycek (Nicholas Lea) perhaps unintentionally foreshadows the ultimate resolution to the mythology when he tells Mulder that there is no "truth" to be found, as the conspirators simply "make it up" along the way. This dialogue is arguably as true of the series' antagonists as it is of the writers. Quite apart from 9/11, some have argued that this was the primary reason for the series' decline.

However, the series' producers were well aware that deferred resolution of the mythology could not continue forever. Efforts were made throughout the broadcast run to address viewer concern with the circuitous nature of the mythology storyline. Although *Fight the Future* was promoted with the tagline, "THE TRUTH IS REVEALED ONLY IN THEATRES," some fans reacted angrily to the perceived dumbing down of the film's storyline for audiences unfamiliar with the show. After a backlash against the marketing of the film, the creators publicly stated that over the following seasons they would finally resolve the series' long-standing questions. Midway through season six, in a two-part episode entitled "Two Fathers/One Son" (itself a reference to Mulder's ambiguous parentage), the series purportedly concluded the mythology storyline by killing off the Syndicate. Importantly though, the series' arch villain, the Cigarette Smoking Man, survived these events and would continue to appear in future episodes including the series finale. While the Cigarette Smoking Man was apparently killed off for the last time in "The Truth" (which graphically depicts his flesh burning off his skull in an explosion), actor William B. Davis is confirmed to play an as yet unknown role in the series' 2016 revival. This demonstrates yet again how the series resists a definitive conclusion to its mythology storyline.

Similarly, in season seven the series claimed to provide a final explanation for the whereabouts of Mulder's sister. Since the series' pilot, Mulder's investigations into the paranormal were motivated by a desire to discover what happened to his missing sister. As with other aspects of the mythology, the storyline of Samantha Mulder's disappearance was subject to numerous competing explanations over the series' run. In "Paper Hearts," a child molester whom Mulder helped to capture teases the agent with information about his sister, suggesting that a more earthly fate (and not aliens) may have been responsible for her abduction. In seasons two and five, we are shown adult versions of Samantha, only for these to later be revealed as clones. When Mulder pleads with the alien bounty hunter in "End Game" to tell him where his sister is, the bounty hunter responds that she is "alive." Likewise, a near-death Mulder has a vision of the afterlife in "The Blessing Way," where a spectral vision of his father states that Samantha is not "here," encouraging him to continue looking. Finally however, the series' producers resolved to conclude this storyline in season seven's "Closure." This episode claims that after Mulder's sister was abducted by aliens as a child, she was returned and died as a teenager in 1979, spirited away 'in starlight.'

Many critics characterised "Closure" as an unexpected (and not altogether successful) attempt to wrap-up the mystery that formed the basis of *The X-Files* since the first episode. Some fans responded unfavourably to this resolution, noting that it directly contradicted previous assurances that Mulder's sister was alive. Indeed, the explanation provided is so ambiguous that it in fact resolves very little. Significantly, later in the season seven finale, "Requiem," Mulder himself acknowledges the unsatisfactory nature of these explanations when he is asked by an FBI auditor to justify the exorbitant cost of his investigations. With the conspiracy now defunct and the mystery of his sister's disappearance apparently solved, the auditor points out that Mulder's investigations seem to have concluded, to which Mulder responds that "nothing" has actually been resolved.

The deferred resolution of the mythology which these examples illustrate clearly grated on some viewers. Indeed, many audience members began to suspect that the producers had no idea where the mythology was heading. The show's production history in later years certainly fuelled these suspicions, as the seventh and eighth season finales were written and filmed before *The X-Files* had been renewed for the following year. One critic lambasted the mythology in later seasons as "ponderous," offering "one supposedly mind-boggling revelation after another," while simultaneously avoiding resolution and failing to answer the many questions posed by the series.[56] But while some have cited the failure to resolve these storylines earlier as a reason for the series' drop in popularity in 2001-02, this neglects the very obvious commercial considerations in continuing the mythology indefinitely.

As noted earlier, *The X-Files'* standalone episodes conform to the definition of a 'series' – they are not interrelated and require little or no knowledge of what has gone before. Conversely, the mythology episodes form part of an overarching storyline, with

---

[56] Vitaris, P. and Coyle, D. "X'd Out" in *Cinefantastique*, Vol. 34, Iss. 2 (April 2002), p. 40.

complex character relationships requiring a detailed knowledge of the events of previous instalments. In this sense, *The X-Files* is an example of a 'hybrid' form – combining elements of both 'series' and 'serial' narratives. Events do not accumulate in the standalone episodes and characters generally do not *learn* from these incidents, instead they forget the events of previous instalments each week. Importantly though, while events can accumulate in the 'serial' form, they can never be fully concluded as this is the nature of the program – the 'serial' narrative can never truly end without ending the show.

Accordingly, the suggestion that *The X-Files'* dramatic decline in ratings after 9/11 was the result of viewer frustration with the mythology's failure to conclude is simplistic – the *purpose* of these episodes was to leave the viewer not quite satisfied, in order to keep them coming back.

Missing Mulder

In 2008, Chris Carter commented that, "We ended the show right about the right time. There was a big change in the country after 9/11."[57] While this statement may indeed be true, it ignores the behind the scenes changes that were occurring to *The X-Files* at that same time. In 2001, between the eighth and ninth seasons, David Duchovny departed the series for good, only returning for the final episode when it was confirmed that the series was drawing to a close.

There can be no doubt that Duchovny's departure, and the corresponding 'disappearance' of Mulder in the series' storylines, greatly affected the program's reception. While Gillian Anderson's character of Scully remained, the series primarily followed the exploits of two new protagonists – Agents John Doggett (Robert Patrick) and Monica Reyes (Annabeth Gish), who were

---

[57] This quotation is transcribed from the "Wondercon Talent Panel" special feature on *The X-Files - Essentials*, a DVD reissue released to coincide with the opening of the second feature film: *The X-Files - Essentials*, Region 4, Disc 2, Twentieth Century Fox Home Entertainment, 2008, DVD.

now assigned to investigate the "x-files." After highly publicised disputes with the series' stars, this reinvention of the show perhaps demonstrates a preference on the part of the broadcaster that the stories, and not the characters themselves, would dictate the future of the series. Indeed, the show's subject matter continued to focus on the paranormal while the introduction of new characters allowed for fresh storylines.

Despite this new direction, a vociferous section of the fan-base decried what they saw as the unnecessary continuation of the show at the hands of greedy network executives. These viewers argued that the series had *always* been about Mulder and Scully. Epitomising this sort of reaction, some argued that they "hoped" the show would end when Duchovny left, as *The X-Files* fundamentally "did not work" without its two leads.[58] However, we should be wary of assuming that statements such as these represent the feelings of all viewers. The audience for any television program is diverse and varied, and it would be a mistake to assume that the mass medium of television is interpreted in the same way by every viewer. While some fans passionately dissected the intricacies of Mulder and Scully's relationship, others protested just as vociferously that the series had always been about their investigations, the stories the show presented, and not the characters private lives.

Although it has been argued that the occurrence of the 9/11 attacks immediately before *The X-Files'* final season alienated much of its viewership, many remain convinced that it was Mulder's simultaneous departure that killed the series. Importantly however, during the eighth season (in which Mulder was abducted by aliens and returned to appear in half the episodes) the show remained Fox's highest rated drama. Indeed, season eight actually *increased* the series' share of the audience from the previous year (probably reflecting the overall decline in television viewer

---

[58] For example, see: Kessenich, T. *Examinations: An Unauthorized Look at Seasons 6-9 of The X-Files*, Trafford, Victoria, 2002, pp. 192-193.

numbers as audiences migrated to cable and other platforms). Of course, viewers that year would have been acutely aware that Mulder would eventually return. The reporting of the stars' contract negotiations became a feature of *The X-Files* in later seasons, with the audience's interest in the series' extratextual elements occasionally rivalling their fascination with the show's own stories.

Therefore, just as the series' viewers were aware in season eight that David Duchovny was contracted to return for half the episodes, they would equally have been aware in the final season that he had left the show indefinitely. Strangely, despite the audience's easy access to the show's casting details and production history, in the 2001-02 season the writers attempted to continue featuring Mulder as a character. While this decision was apparently made to allow the character to return in subsequent feature films, the ninth season's storylines suffered as a result. Despite being physically absent, episodes continued to revolve around Mulder and the possibility of his return. The season premiere, "Nothing Important Happened Today," shows an obscured figure (apparently Mulder) showering in Scully's apartment preparing to go into hiding. Another such example, "Trust No 1," teased the possibility of Mulder's return from hiding, utilising archival footage and an extreme long-shot of a stand-in playing the character. Many reviews of the final season have identified the problems with this type of storytelling – with viewers well aware that one of the lead actors had now departed, such storylines represented an exercise in futility. The series could no longer credibly suggest that Mulder would return, but at the same time the writers were reluctant to kill off the character for fear of jeopardising future storylines.

There is no denying that the final season of *The X-Files* was greatly impacted by the loss of one of its main stars. However if this were the *sole* reason for the series' decline in popularity, one would expect the series finale in which David Duchovny appeared to have increased ratings back to their previous heights. While the series had once regularly attracted over 20 million viewers in the U.S., the final episode (featuring Duchovny) was viewed by just 13.6 million people. Even some season eight episodes in which Duchovny had not appeared garnered bigger audiences. Similarly, if the absence of Duchovny was the only reason for the final season's ratings decline, one would have expected *I Want to Believe*, widely trumpeted as the 'reunion' of Mulder and Scully, to have performed well at the box office. In the end, that movie was unable to even recoup its production budget domestically, with box office grosses in the U.S. totalling less than a quarter of the first film. Although Mulder's presence was obviously important, these examples demonstrate that even those instalments that did feature the character after 9/11 struggled to find an audience. This suggests that it was an event far beyond the producers' control that ultimately killed *The X-Files*.

CONCLUSION

Many commentators note the incongruity of *The X-Files'* subversive politics and the more traditional views of its parent company. Academics frequently analyse the Fox network alongside its owner, conservative media mogul Rupert Murdoch, as if all production is personally overseen by the company's major shareholder. It has even been argued elsewhere that *The X-Files* was an attack by Rupert Murdoch's media empire on 'big' government in the 1990s. But the extent to which the politics of the franchise reflect those of its parent company are debatable. Although News Corporation's media outlets are often pilloried for their jingoistic and militaristic content (particularly Fox News), *The X-Files* is an example of a text which bucks this trend.

In the mid-nineties, the series fed perfectly into the American public's unease following the Cold War, playing on fears about the unrestrained growth of U.S. military power. The show frequently depicts military personnel in peril – whether being assassinated by an invisible Vietnam veteran in "Unrequited," or tormented by a voodoo curse in "Fresh Bones." Such content is hardly consistent with the patriotic hyperbole usually associated with Rupert Murdoch's media outlets. For this reason, we must be wary of equating the political views of a television text with those of its owner. Control or ownership in the media does not necessarily indicate the political orientation of a particular program. Nevertheless, it is tempting to speculate what effect 9/11 might have had on Fox's opinion of *The X-Files*. Robert Patrick, the actor who served as the 'replacement' for David Duchovny in the series' final two years, publicly criticised the network's perceived privileging of its new series, *24*, after 9/11. Following the conclusion of the show, Patrick questioned Fox's promotional strategy, recalling that he felt *The X-Files* had been "abandoned" by the network.[59] Is it possible that following 9/11, the same News Corporation which had previously exploited *The X-Files'* popularity for commercial gain found itself in stark disagreement with the politics of the series?

As we have seen, the series' initial popularity in the wake of the Cold War makes perfect sense – in the absence of an identifiable, external enemy, the audience's fears were internalised to reflect an increasing distrust of government. But when a common enemy emerged once again following 9/11, the 'us' and 'them' distinction that characterised the Cold War returned once more. Following the terror attacks, the media's previous ambivalence towards the Bush administration immediately evaporated, as the U.S. networks quickly began broadcasting patriotic messages of support amid declarations that America was now at war. Criticism or opposition to U.S. policy was largely absent from the mainstream media, as citizens looked to their government for leadership.

Yet in this environment, *The X-Files* continued to engage in explicit criticism of government. The series' ninth season premiere, "Nothing Important Happened Today" (produced before 9/11 but aired several months after), provides an illuminating example. The narrative of the episode deals with a government experiment, stretching back to the Gulf War, to turn the population into super-soldiers by tainting the water supply. In hindsight, this episode provides an ironic commentary on the media's championing of the march to war, as well as demonstrating a remarkable

---

[59] Robert Patrick quoted in: Hurwitz, M. & Knowles, C. *The Complete X-Files: Behind the Series, the Myths, and the Movies*, Insight Editions, San Rafael, 2008, p. 206.

prescience, two years before the U.S. would once again go to war in Iraq. Although such subject matter should have gained greater relevance following 9/11, the show failed to find an audience in its final year.

The X-Files' stories were arguably even more topical in an age where the U.S. government sought to strip civil liberties and centralise power within the executive. Others have noted eerie similarities between the series' content and the post-9/11 anthrax scares, where officials in hazmat suits where shown decontaminating buildings.[60] However it is understandable that viewers witnessing such images on the nightly news might shun similar scenes in a dramatic series. Clearly then the momentous events of this date irrevocably changed the zeitgeist of society. So monumental was the effect of 9/11, that studios and television producers appeared unwilling or unable to deal with the gravity of the events in the aftermath of the disaster. Hollywood largely focused on producing either apolitical genre pictures, or otherwise promoted family films and comedies to distract Americans from real-life events. In this way, it appears that there was an overwhelming urge in Hollywood *not* to address 9/11 so soon after the attacks.

This same creative atrophy is evident in *The X-Files* episodes produced after 9/11. We have already seen that realism and immediacy were features of the series, and indeed terrorism often featured in the show's narratives. For example, in "Space" when the agents investigate a possible saboteur within NASA, Scully questions why someone would want to sabotage the space shuttle. Mulder's response eerily predicts the symbolic nature of the 9/11 targets, noting that for potential terrorists the space shuttle would be an icon of U.S. "progress and prosperity." Another early episode shows Scully discussing how a fellow FBI agent was promoted after investigating the World Trade Centre bombing.

---

[60] For example, see: Cantor, P.A. "The Truth Is Still Out There: *The X-Files* and 9/11" in *Homer Simpson Marches on Washington – Dissent through American Popular Culture* (Ed. Timothy M. Dale and Joseph J. Foy), The University Press of Kentucky, Lexington, 2010, pp. 75-96.

But in the face of 9/11, this series which had previously presented stories in a recognisably real world, incorporating visual details and storytelling devices to ground the narrative within our own shared history, refused to acknowledge that circumstances had changed. Post-9/11, *The X-Files* steadfastly neglected to address the fallout from the attacks, apparently acknowledging that to do so would be an affront to victims of the tragedy. In fact, apart from an extratextual dedication, the series never explicitly referenced 9/11 at all ("Nothing Important Happened Today II" is dedicated to Chad Keller, a friend of series creator Chris Carter and victim of the terrorist attacks). When Doggett goes missing in the final season episode, "John Doe," Scully is told that extra agents cannot be devoted to the search because FBI resources are taxed by issues of "national security" in a rare acknowledgement of the changed political climate. Importantly, the series' final episode *was* to conclude with a scene showing President George W. Bush being debriefed about efforts to find Mulder and Scully, however the scene was cut.[61] Clearly, the public attitude at the time played a part in the decision to excise this scene from the broadcast version. Aside from some oblique references, with the trauma of the attacks so fresh in the public's mind, *The X-Files* perhaps understandably chose to avoid the subject of 9/11 altogether.

If the series' refusal to deal with 9/11 is indicative of a broader trend within mainstream U.S. film and television to ignore the attacks in their immediate aftermath, it is also consistent with *The X-Files'* balancing of its own political rhetoric. As we have seen, although the series engaged in overt criticism of governmental authority, the writers were careful never to appear partisan. Although the series depicted subversive content such as citizens manipulated by an unelected shadow government, it also foregrounded the futility of Mulder and Scully's resistance to this

---

[61] This deleted scene is available as a special feature on *The X-Files'* season nine DVD release: *The X-Files: The Complete Ninth Season*, Region 4, Disc 6, Twentieth Century Fox Home Entertainment, 2004, DVD.

conspiracy – when Mulder finally learns the date of the alien invasion in the ninth season finale, he admits defeat, stating that the date has been "set," and he cannot change it. In this sense, Carter's claim that the show was never intended to be "revolutionary" rings true. Despite *The X-Files'* apparently subversive political view, there was always a tension between what the series could (and could not) get away with. While it pushed boundaries, *The X-Files* was nevertheless restricted by the need to be a commercially viable product, acceptable to a mainstream audience. For example, the program's often gruesome subject matter still had to conform to what its broadcaster believed was suitable. Therefore, for much of its lifespan the series was able to offer fresh content in the form of conspiracies and fantastic storylines, whilst remaining accessible enough not to be dismissed as paranoid garbage.

Post-9/11, though, the series struggled to tread this fine line between subversion and acceptability. In "Terma," Scully is held in contempt of Congress for refusing to divulge information to a Senate Subcommittee on Intelligence and Terrorism. By the show's final season though, real-life events had rendered such storylines unpalatable for a country on high alert. Still overtly critical of government, but unwilling to incorporate any of the realism and immediacy which had previously been tolerated for fear of offending the country in the wake of such a traumatic event, *The X-Files* was creatively hamstrung. The zeitgeist of the U.S. had been abruptly and irrevocably altered by the attacks and although the producers tried to change the series' approach to its subject matter, nothing could alter the series' well-established reputation for provocative storylines and subversive content.

Chris Carter acknowledged during the final season that, "We lost our audience on the first episode. It's like the audience had gone away and I didn't know how to find them."[62] While it is tempting

---

[62] Chris Carter quoted in: Goodman, T. "*X-Files'* creator ends Fox series," *San Francisco Chronicle*, 18 January 2002. Retrieved from: http://www.sfgate.com/entertainment/article/X-Files-creator-ends-Fox-series-2883631.php (accessed 23 September 2015).

to speculate about whether or not *The X-Files* fell victim to media attacks in the wake of 9/11, or perhaps was intentionally sabotaged by its own network, there is precious little evidence for either of these scenarios. Instead, it seems that the series' audience simply tuned out – traumatised and disaffected by the events of 9/11, most people were no longer willing to engage in criticism of the authorities that they now relied on for protection.

Ultimately, this book has argued that *The X-Files'* demise was primarily attributable to the extremely conservative atmosphere which pervaded the U.S. population immediately following 9/11. Serious social and political debate was absent in the immediate aftermath as citizens put their faith and trust in the government for protection, and retribution for the attacks. While it may be easy to dismiss this fervour as a short-term response to an extraordinary event, the reception of *I Want to Believe* – released seven years after 9/11 – appeared to confirm that the events of September 2001 marked the definitive end of *The X-Files'* era. Although that film was ostensibly an apolitical genre story, it nevertheless incorporated the series' distinctive atmosphere of foreboding and unease. In one scene, Mulder and Scully return to the FBI (having been in hiding since the end of the series) where they are confronted with adjacent portraits of George W. Bush and J. Edgar Hoover. A threatening musical cue plays, drawing implicit connections between the FBI's fevered response to "un-American activities" under Hoover, and the Bush administration's equally rabid pursuit of "enemies of freedom." Despite the fact that this latent political comment accompanied a prolonged trough in the then President's approval rating, it did not assist the film to find a significant audience. In contrast to the 1990s when *The X-Files* was at the height of its popularity, by the time of the second film's release in 2008 the U.S. had undergone tremendous upheaval (the most obvious manifestation of which was the country's renewed military engagement, on several fronts). There can be little doubt that *The X-Files'* era, characterised by the social, political and economic uncertainty that accompanied the end of the Cold War (along with a relatively permissive environment under the Clinton administration), had definitively ended on 9/11. Nevertheless, the series still retains contemporary relevance, remaining an example of an intelligent television series that will forever provide a compelling insight into the period in which it was broadcast.

Part II

Revisiting *The X-Files*

SEASON ONE

The interesting thing about the first season is how many features of the show had already crystallised by this early stage. Vancouver's contribution to the series' signature atmosphere is already evident from the first few frames of the **Pilot**. Chris Carter's intelligent writing is assisted by Duchovny and Anderson's strong portrayals (even if Mulder does seem a little more hyperactive than usual here). Other aspects aren't quite as successful, including some uneven supporting performances. Perhaps understandably, at this early stage Mark Snow's score offers only subtle hints of what will follow (the absence of the main theme and title sequence is particularly noticeable). Overall though, the first episode is a strong early entry to the canon.

The most admirable aspect of **Deep Throat** is the fact that Mulder and Scully are placed in real danger at such an early stage of the series' run. Scully's rescue of her partner at gunpoint also cements her role as an active heroine, and not just a passive sounding board for her male partner. It's also impressive how well some of these special effects hold up after so many years.

Squeeze is particularly noteworthy for demonstrating that the series would not be dealing exclusively with UFOs and aliens. Although the 'monsters of the week' understandably varied in quality over the years, Glen Morgan & James Wong's debut proves that with good writing, strong performances and some imagination, the series only needs to suggest a little and the audience's fear of the unknown will fill in the blanks.

While **Conduit** suffers from some poor plotting and confusing lapses in logic, it is an enjoyable enough viewing experience thanks to some interesting images. Referencing Samantha's own disappearance is the best aspect here, anchoring these events in the context of the series' broader narrative. On the other hand, the whole device of Kevin receiving signals through the television leads precisely nowhere. It's a fairly inconsequential entry, but it succeeds by making the audience believe that these events could be more important than they really are.

The Jersey Devil is perhaps the first noticeable drop in quality, demonstrating that the gruelling nature of a network television production schedule can take its toll. Mulder's almost sexual fascination with the 'beast woman' and ranting about missing links adds up to very little. The police captain's outright contempt for Mulder continues these early episodes' tradition of painting law enforcement as hopelessly wracked by infighting and opportunism (a device the series would thankfully employ more sparingly in the future). Some of these early entries, including **Shadows**, display quite obvious signs of network interference (Scully's date in 'The Jersey Devil,' and the overwhelming focus on 'relatable' office workers in 'Shadows'). This lack of creative flair and routine story consigns 'Shadows' to the status of a noble failure, despite the presence of some pretty cool visuals. While it is perhaps understandable that the network would attempt to shepherd a series in its infancy, to Fox's credit the creators would later be afforded greater freedom.

Ghost in the Machine is one episode that received a lot of hate at the time of its broadcast, but it feels like it has improved with age. The acting and directing are impressive, serving to gloss over some of the weaknesses in the script. While the computer references *are* terribly dated, at its best this serves as a kind of time capsule for a simpler age. Today, where mobile technology has pervaded nearly aspect of our lives, it's interesting to look back at an episode where the villain is the most static object possible – a building. While parts of the story are certainly derivative, the finale is able to deliver some tense moments.

Ice is almost unanimously regarded as a series classic, establishing the template for numerous episodes that would follow. *The X-Files* would go back to the well of 'Mulder and Scully isolated and in peril' a few times over the years, but the series never quite managed to replicate the gripping tension on offer here. The crackling script is assisted by stellar performances all round, including those of the strong supporting cast.

Space, on the other hand, is an outright disappointment. While it is often said that the series' weakest entries at least look good, that is not the case here. For what was reportedly a very expensive hour of television, this episode *looks* cheap, and the visuals are not assisted by a yawn-inducing narrative. It's interesting to note that this episode's antagonist (the 'face' on Mars) has since been revealed as a trick of light and shadow, just as Colonel Belt claims in the teaser. It only adds to the feeling that this whole story has been a very hollow exercise indeed.

It's refreshing to enjoy the conspiracy-heavy atmosphere of **Fallen Angel** in hindsight, before the dense intricacies of the mythology rendered one-off episodes like this all but impossible. It's actually the third episode in a row to feature an alien presence that will never be seen or heard from again, but the invisible creature leads to some fun scenes (especially the ambush at the microwave substation). For all its action set-pieces though, nothing can top this episode's glorious final scene with Deep Throat for intrigue.

Eve is a little gem of a story with so many red herrings and misdirections that it's easy to forget how brilliant it is once you know the final twist. Everything from vampires, to UFOs, to copycat serial killers is thrown up as a possibility, but the 'creepy kids' (a hallmark of this series) ultimately hold the answers. The casting in this episode is terrific, with the young and old Eves delivering pitch-perfect performances. While this entry is occasionally over-looked, it foreshadows some of the series' best stories that will go on to present a mystery that seems routine at first, only to won-derfully subvert audience expectations.

The great practical effects in **Fire** are unfortunately serviced by a poor story. Phoebe Green's character might have been interesting had she not been written so thinly (why exactly is she making out with the man she's been charged with protecting?), but it certainly doesn't help that Amanda Pays and David Duchovny share no chemistry whatsoever. This is one of those entries where we know exactly who the killer is from the teaser, and we get to spend the rest of the episode watching the characters figure it out.

Beyond the Sea features strangulations, abductions and torture, but it's telling that the opening teaser is the scariest scene. Brad Dourif delivers a standout performance, even though Mark Snow's talents seem strangely underutilised for such a personal story. The 'role reversal' device of Mulder as sceptic and Scully as believer would occasionally wear thin in future, but it proves a fresh and welcome addition at this stage of the show's first season.

Rob Bowman's strong direction adds some wonderful imagery to **Genderbender**, but scratch the surface hoping for a compelling story and you'll be left wanting. By contrasting the sexual excesses of (then) modern nightclubs, and the buttoned-down traditions of the Kindred community, it at first appears that this entry might have something interesting to say. In the end though, it com-pletely avoids making any statement on the preceding events with its fumbling and evasive excuse for an ending.

Lazarus feels a bit more like a standard cop show than an episode of *The X-Files*. That's not necessarily a criticism, but the result is that those aspects of the story that are more supernatural (like the disappearing and reappearing tattoo) feel a little forced. You get the feeling the story might have been stronger without these visual clues, leaving open the possibility that Willis' 'reincarnation' could actually have a more mundane explanation.

Young at Heart is a strange little instalment, with lots of competing elements that are interesting in isolation but don't really come together properly. This entry contains some very stylised sequences – the opening perspective shot from Crandall's wheelchair, Barnett stalking Scully in her apartment, and pretty much the entire climax in the concert hall. Ultimately though, the muddled plot results in a pretty unsatisfying episode.

Aside from a handful of the establishing stories, **E.B.E.** is one of the few first season instalments that really feels like it can take its place as part of the show's broader mythology. This episode also establishes the Lone Gunmen in a great little scene which, unlike some of their later appearances, feels natural and isn't just playing for laughs (Frohike has just two lines!). The idea of alien bodies being transported cross-country is very cool, as summed up in Mulder's comment about the oblivious cars passing this truck by on the highway. It's not quite perfect, but it is noteworthy for showing the potential of the mythology storyline at this early stage.

Like many of *The X-Files'* episodes that deal with religion, **Miracle Man** tries so hard to be respectful and even-handed that it comes across as a little dull. Although it features a few arresting images – the parishioners marching through the graveyard by torchlight and Samuel's crucifix silhouette as he is beaten to death – it ultimately feels a bit hollow. Later standalone shows will demonstrate that the Samantha storyline is not solely the domain of the mythology, but it just seems tacked on here.

Episodes set in the isolated wilderness like **Darkness Falls** are only as strong as the performances, but thankfully everyone here delivers. Utilising the same formula as 'Ice,' 'Darkness Falls' is thankfully able to showcase the value of its Vancouver shooting location in a way that the earlier entry couldn't. The drearily beautiful setting contributes immeasurably to this show's tense atmosphere. It's a shame then that the great build-up is let down by a pretty unsatisfying conclusion, but it's still a rollicking adventure.

The series will bring back other 'monsters of the week' in subsequent seasons, but none as successfully as **Tooms**. Unlike others who will make a second appearance in the future, Tooms feels like a villain who truly *deserved* another bow and his second episode delivers. Mitch Pileggi shines in his first appearance as Skinner, and it's quite sweet to look back and see the series' arch villain, the Cigarette Smoking Man, taking an interest in a run-of-the-mill liver eating mutant as he does here.

Like 'Lazarus,' **Born Again** feels just a bit too much like a standard cop show. Aside from a few good set pieces, the premise of a supernatural revenge story is just too familiar to get excited about. **Roland** deals with very similar subject matter to 'Born Again,' but Zeljko Ivanek's great performance (ably assisted by Mark Snow's fantastic score) is able to elevate the material above that episode. While the performances are incredibly earnest, the direction seems to have a bit more of a sense of humour, with some of the deaths handled in very tongue-in-cheek fashion. In the end though, and not for the first time this season, Mulder and Scully just aren't given enough to do in this story.

Only at the end of the first season does the series start to reveal pieces of the puzzle that will form part of the larger storyline in coming years. **The Erlenmeyer Flask** represents the show's first *true* mythology episode. The killing of Deep Throat and closing down of the x-files feel incredibly risky and shocking, particularly because you get the distinct impression that Carter himself isn't entirely sure how each of these story elements will fit together. It's produced with such energy and flair though that it's hard not to be impressed.

The first season admirably manages to find, and define, the show's signature tone quickly. It is also noteworthy that despite these episodes' age, they still hold up extremely well without appearing too dated. Some stories don't feel very consequential at this early stage – this is the only season without a two-parter – and it's easy to view Mulder and Scully as mere observers watching the mystery unfold during quite a few of these entries. Perhaps it is this simplicity, where viewers could dip in and out each week with no prior knowledge of the series' increasingly complicated backstory, that is one of the reasons why many casual viewers remember these early episodes so fondly.

There are some notable lapses in quality at different points, but this can probably be explained by the creative team taking time to settle in. Chris Carter's contribution to the series obviously goes without saying, but credit for the consistent *feel* of these stories should also go to the series' original writing teams, with Glen Morgan & James Wong, along with Howard Gordon & Alex Gansa, contributing significantly in this regard. While the writing staff remained fairly consistent, there was a large number of guest directors this year. David Nutter would thankfully go on to become a regular contributor to the series, along with Rob Bowman. The series' executive producer, R.W. Goodwin, would also direct most of the premiere and finale episodes shot in Vancouver. The first season's prevalence of one-time writers and directors no doubt contributes to some of the dramatic shifts in tone between these episodes. Once the series had established a stable writing and directing staff in future years, many of these issues would be resolved.

SEASON TWO

The second season opens with Mulder and Scully in a pretty dark place, but **Little Green Men** revels in this conspiracy-heavy atmosphere and the overwhelming sense of unease it creates for the audience. This entry could have been fairly dispiriting, but it actually feels like the perfect way to pick up proceedings after 'The Erlenmeyer Flask.' Looking back, it's easy to forget how momentous some of these events – seeing Samantha's abduction and our first grey alien – were at the beginning of the second season.

The Host takes all the elements of a B-movie and manages to fashion them into something that seems somehow more sophisticated than the sum of its parts. The flukeman is one villain that has rightly entered series folklore, and it's easy to see why given how tense and terrific this episode is. The series was growing in stature at this stage, but this episode proves that sometimes the most straightforward monster stories are the best. **Blood**, meanwhile, tries hard to cram in a lot of interesting ideas, but none are really given enough attention. In a series known for leaving questions unresolved, 'Blood' stretches credulity a bit too far with its abrupt ending. It also feels like a missed opportunity to examine some of the darker aspects of American paranoia and gun culture in detail.

Sleepless proves a directorial tour de force from Rob Bowman, with gloriously cinematic images abounding. The episode is greatly assisted by Howard Gordon's great central premise, and strong performances all round. Particularly noteworthy are Nicholas Lea and Steven Williams in their first appearances as Krycek and X – two characters who would rightly go on to become fan favourites.

Although it at first seems like a tense, self-contained story, **Duane Barry** essentially establishes the series' overarching mythology. Scully's abduction (necessitated by Gillian Anderson's pregnancy) would go on to become one of *The X-Files'* narrative touchstones over the years. In his directorial debut, Chris Carter garners some strong performances from his cast, and the series' first cliffhanger is suitably shocking.

Following on from 'Duane Barry,' **Ascension** is perhaps an underrated instalment. Without the high-concept hostage drama of its predecessor, this episode's sole purpose is to allow Scully (missing when the episode begins) to be abducted by aliens. What is impressive is that it manages to elicit real tension from this scenario, holding out the possibility that Mulder may actually prevent her abduction. Skinner and the Cigarette Smoking Man's appearances are welcome additions, and as usual this entry's atmosphere owes much to some stunning Vancouver locations.

As one of the few entries not to feature Scully at all, **3** is nobody's favourite episode. You can see what the creators were trying to do by having Mulder go off on this melancholy journey, but the central storyline of kinky vampires is just not interesting enough to hold the viewer's attention.

Capping off an unofficial trilogy that began with 'Duane Barry'/'Ascension,' **One Breath** is close to perfection. Glen Morgan & James Wong's dialogue crackles to the point where you hardly notice that the episode takes place almost entirely within a hospital while one of the main characters is comatose. The hint of menace and paranoia with which Steven Williams has portrayed X pays off in spades here, with one brilliant sequence showcasing the potential of this character. Duchovny's performance will rarely be better than the one he delivers here.

Firewalker very abruptly returns the agents to their usual roles and, not for the last time, some fans were disappointed that the characters barely acknowledge the enormity of recent events. Nevertheless, it *is* refreshing to see Mulder and Scully once again investigating cases, even if this particular story bears a striking resemblance to previous entries. Derivative or not, 'Firewalker' functions well as a tense bottle story, best viewed in isolation.

Red Museum at first presents itself as a run-of-the-mill story, before morphing quite quickly into a conspiracy episode. By having a bet each way like this, the story never really shines as either a 'monster of the week' or a mythology entry. Despite the fact that the plot relies far too heavily on coincidences, it's still perfectly watchable without soaring to any great heights.

The central premise of 'spectral rape' in **Excelsius Dei** is interesting. It contains some good set-pieces, but the proceedings feel a little hollow by the end as Mulder and Scully's involvement ultimately achieves very little. It doesn't help that the characters, whether it's Mulder dismissing the victim of a sexual assault, the orderlies, or even some of the residents themselves, are entirely unsympathetic.

A welcome horror entry, **Aubrey** has a great atmosphere and delivers some solid shocks. The early scenes are appropriately chilling, but once the mystery is revealed the story fizzles out a bit by the end. Conversely, while we know the killer's true identity before the opening credits roll in **Irresistible**, the episode manages to maintain its chilling atmosphere with an excellent performance from Nick Chinlund. Although placing Scully in jeopardy may occasionally seem gratuitous in future, witnessing her struggle with her emotions makes the climax all the more powerful here.

Die Hand Die Verletzt is a strange little episode, with flashes of black comedy amidst the strange goings on. This tongue-in-cheek approach works pretty well to soften the shocking images on display, but one wonders whether the episode would have worked better if it had jettisoned the satire in favour of a creepier tone. **Fresh Bones** certainly subscribes to the latter approach, and it manages to elevate what would otherwise be a pretty ordinary episode above the schlocky material. While pretty much every characters' motivations are unclear, the strong performances are enough for the viewer to ignore the script's deficiencies.

With **Colony**, it feels for the first time like the writers are *intentionally* developing a broader mythology. Some familiar sights return (beings suspended in tanks of green goo), along with some cool new imagery like the shape-shifting bounty hunter and his stiletto. The cliffhanger is a pretty good one, but **End Game** seems to meander until reaching its admittedly impressive climax. Mulder's admission to his father that he lost his sister again so soon after her return is strangely underplayed (for reasons that are only made clear later). With the benefit of hindsight, having Samantha return so early in the series' run now seems like a misstep, serving only to lessen the impact of this device in future.

The opening of **Fearful Symmetry** is visually impressive, but once the investigation gets going the script's weaknesses become apparent. This is one of the last times where vaguely defined goals are attributed to unseen beings from another world, before aliens became strictly the domain of the mythology. Given how dull much of this episode is, it's probably for the best.

Død Kalm revives the familiar concept of isolating Mulder and Scully in a remote location. As with similar stories, it is the discussions and interactions between the pair that are the episode's biggest strengths. It's a fairly strong entry overall, but, just as with 'Darkness Falls,' the atmosphere of foreboding that is developed so assiduously over the first few acts is undercut by the cop-out of an ending.

Darin Morgan's arrival with **Humbug** showed for the first time that this normally straight series could occasionally poke fun at itself. Unlike some of Morgan's later entries, there is a charming innocence to this story. Whether one considers the deeper subtexts or not, it is very easy to be amused by the craziness on display in 'Humbug.'

The Calusari is a return to the first season staple of 'creepy kid' stories (see 'Conduit,' 'Eve,' 'Born Again'). The provocative teaser in which a toddler is killed demonstrates the series' increasing self-assurance and ability to push boundaries. As usual, it is expertly produced and the actors all deliver strong performances, but after a while the latent criticism of foreign cultures in this one becomes a bit too much bear.

F. Emasculata benefits from one of Howard Gordon's finest scripts, proving that the show's great effects and strong perform- ances are more than just skin-deep. Rob Bowman's cinematic visuals here also foreshadow the feature film one more than one occasion. The conspiracy machinations can become a little confus- ing by the end, but it is always fun to see the characters squaring off so intimately with the Cigarette Smoking Man.

While it could otherwise be dismissed as pretty routine, **Soft Light** is notable for marking the debut of one of the series' best writers. The 'killer shadow' demonstrates Vince Gilligan's flair for an imaginative premise, although he would shrewdly drop most of the conspiracy and sci-fi elements from his future contributions.

Aside from a few evergreen residents, there are very few para- normal goings on in **Our Town**. The mystery itself is pretty good, but the wheels fall off a little by the end. Putting Scully in danger is lazy enough, but the 'twist' in the episode's climax is also totally unnecessary. Revealing the executioner's identity makes very little sense to the rest of the plot, and it's one of the few times where the series missed an opportunity for an ambiguous ending.

While 'Colony' dabbled with Cold War paranoia as a red herring, **Anasazi** marks the first time that *The X-Files* began intermingling real-life events with the series' own backstory. The revelations about Mulder's family are handled well, although some of Albert Hosteen's dialogue about 'mysteries wanting to be revealed' seems very heavy-handed. The long final scene (ably assisted by Mark Snow's score) ranks as one of the series' best cliffhangers, even if it is never satisfactorily explained.

By season two, The X-Files had begun to enter the mainstream consciousness. The quality of these episodes is remarkable given the sheer length of the season and the gruelling network schedule. While the second season does feature the odd misstep, the sense of momentum is palpable – the first tentative steps of the mythology episodes here feel like they are building to something bigger, and they're exciting to watch.

David Duchovny and Gillian Anderson have clearly become comfortable in their roles by this stage, so it's good to see them both getting some more challenging material this year. The increasing prevalence of supporting players like Mitch Pileggi and Steven Williams also demonstrates the potential for the ensemble cast to play a greater role in the future.

Behind the scenes, Glen Morgan & James Wong departed after contributing so much to the establishment of the show's tone, while this season also saw a number of significant additions. Frank Spotnitz would go on to be crucial to the development of the series' mythology, while Vince Gilligan (who contributed a spec script, but elected not to join the staff) would become arguably the series' most creative scribe. Kim Manners also entered the directors' stable this year, joining R.W. Goodwin, David Nutter and Rob Bowman. There can be little doubt that the show's success in following seasons owes much to the consistency and stability of the creative team established this year.

SEASON THREE

Airing between two fine episodes, **The Blessing Way** suffers by comparison. The 'blink and you'll miss it' explanation for Mulder's escape from the boxcar leaves much to be desired (a small hole in the wall is barely visible during the gassing flashback), and his near-death visions are equally unsatisfying. The discovery of a chip in Scully's neck throws up some nice questions, but this plot point is quickly forgotten by the following episode. Ultimately, as with many of these middle acts in a trilogy, this one feels like it's in a holding pattern... It's a good thing, then, that **Paper Clip** delivers. The unequivocal statement of U.S. government collusion with Nazi scientists is a fascinating idea, and the scenes at the mine are genuinely gripping. Rob Bowman's glorious visuals certainly prove worthy of this script's lofty ideas. Skinner has some great lines, and it's good to see Mulder and Scully uncovering these mysteries *together* for a change. Too often, the pair get split up during these mythology episodes simply to allow for more exposition.

D.P.O. marks a return to the series' usual standalone fare. While some viewers apparently had a problem with Mulder and Scully returning to routine investigations after the revelations of the previous episode, it's unfair to single out this specific episode when such complaints are really criticising the nature of the series itself. Along with 'creepy kids,' 'angsty teens' are another *X-Files* staple. The plot may frankly be a little run-of-the-mill (especially the uncooperative Sheriff character who we've seen many times before), but some great sequences and the breakout performances of Giovanni Ribisi and Jack Black really elevate this entry.

At this point, I must confess something that I understand will not endear me to many readers – I really dislike **Clyde Bruckman's Final Repose**. I am aware that the Emmy Award-winning episode is critically acclaimed and is often singled out as many people's favourite. Peter Boyle undoubtedly gives an excellent performance as the tortured clairvoyant, but I personally find Darin Morgan's script incredibly grating. Almost every line in the episode is a misdirect, with characters made to seem like they are referring to one thing when they are in fact referring to another. By the time Bruckman greets Mulder sight unseen, describes the investigation in great detail, and then acts surprised to see him (a line of dialogue that *consciously* leads nowhere), my patience for this material has been exhausted. It's not that I can't appreciate the different levels this episode is operating on, it's just that I can't connect with it emotionally at all.

The List epitomises those X-Files episodes that look great, but are let down by a weak script. Creator Chris Carter bears responsibility in this case for both the compellingly atmospheric look, and the script's deficiencies. J.T. Walsh delivers a great supporting performance, and the prison set is magnificent. But with so much death on offer, this script gives us no reason to care about any of these characters. By the end, we can only join Mulder and Scully in scratching our heads, wondering what the point of it all was.

2Shy and **The Walk** form a pair of satisfying, creepy monster episodes. The former is a solid riff on 'Squeeze,' with the monster requiring human fat tissue rather than livers for survival. What distinguishes this episode from simply being a tired rehash is the sadistic *modus operandi* of Virgil Incanto. Unlike Tooms' monosyllabic mutant, here we have an all too human lothario preying on vulnerable women. The internet discussions seem a little dated now, but it's a solid little horror story. Similarly, 'The Walk' offers some good scares, and is immeasurably assisted in this regard by Rob Bowman's great imagery. Some of the content here is so incredibly dark – the murder of the General's son, and the almost flippant way in which his wife's death is handled – that it's amazing to consider how it got past the censors. The sequence where the disembodied soldier stalks his victim in the pool is a stand-out for the season and, perhaps, the entire series.

A young girl is abducted at the beginning of **Oubliette**, and the strongest parts of the episode directly address the parallels between this case and the disappearance of Mulder's own sister. Especially satisfying is Mulder's outburst about how his emotions can't all be connected back to Samantha's disappearance (apparently an *ad lib* from Duchovny), with this acknowledgement serving to make him a much more rounded character. At times Charles Grant Craig's script (his only credit for the series) meanders a little, but the forests around Vancouver prove their worth yet again, giving the episode a wonderful, solemn atmosphere.

Following revelations of the conspiracy's collusion with Nazis, **Nisei** and **731** take the logical next step of implicating Japanese war criminals in efforts to create a human/alien hybrid. 'Nisei' propels along quite well, using the conceit of an alien/human hybrid that we have seen before (and will see again). But it is '731' which has the tougher job of making two characters trapped in a train car compelling. The episode achieves this by switching the focus to depictions of death squads and mass graves in the backwoods of modern-day America – images as chilling and subversive as anything the series will ever deliver. '731' also succeeds in establishing a counter-narrative for Scully that is at once more credible and insidious than Mulder's belief in aliens or UFOs. Arguably two of the series' finest mythology entries.

An intelligent examination of Scully's faith (and Mulder's disdain for organised religion) proves to be the biggest strength of **Revelations**. Reversing the usual sceptic/believer roles works here, unlike some subsequent episodes where it can begin to feel forced. The rest of the plot leaves a bit to be desired, with Kevin's character, his miraculous abilities and the killer's motives all defined in only the vaguest terms.

There are some fun jokes and interesting ideas in **War of the Coprophages**, particularly the themes of mass panic, but the over-arching story is a little tenuous. Some of the dialogue really sparkles (especially the scenes between Duchovny and Anderson), so it's such a shame that the episode doesn't seem to know what to do with the central cockroach narrative. Darin Morgan's script was reportedly delivered under significant time constraints and, while it definitely shows potential, it looks like it could have used another polish.

Much like last season's 'Die Hand Die Verletzt,' there is a jarring disconnect between the attempts at comedy in **Syzgy** and the images of teenagers being horrifically killed. Part of this can be attributed to the direction, which certainly focuses more on the horror than it does the comedy. Black comedy is okay, and the terse interplay between Mulder and Scully is certainly amusing, but at times the characters' behaviour just comes across as insensitive given the tragedies occurring on-screen.

Grotesque revisits the psychological thriller genre that the series did so well in 'Beyond the Sea.' John Bartley's cinematography is excellent, with cool blues and rich blacks filling every corner of the frame. The script is also pretty good, even if the audience never quite accepts that Mulder could really become a serial killer during the middle of a season. This is an incredibly dark episode, but the tone feels more than appropriate for the story. Some of the murders, and especially Mulder's dreams, are as frightening as anything the series has done before.

The black oil introduced in **Piper Maru** will go on to become a central tenet of *The X-Files'* mythology. It's interesting that the writers themselves seem to be unaware of just how important this thread is to the mythology, with the radioactivity element employed here quickly forgotten about for five seasons. Likewise, the suggestion in **Apocrypha** that the black oil is simply ordinary diesel oil is dropped altogether in future episodes. It *is* about time that the series dealt with the death of Scully's sister, and Krycek's return is always welcome. The scale of these episodes is what's most impressive, convincingly depicting locations as diverse as the Pacific Ocean, North Dakota, San Francisco and Washington D.C. (Hong Kong doesn't get a whole lot of screen-time, except for one corridor and an anonymous airport). The best mythology episodes usually have at least one memorable set-piece, and the missile silo climax continues this tradition.

Pusher is arguably the best stand-alone episode of what is one of the best seasons of the show. Vince Gilligan's writing is dripping with great exchanges, and there is a welcome focus on the characters. The central idea of an antagonist who is able to 'push' his will onto others seems so simple, but the execution is utterly compelling. The setup can really only lead to one outcome – a showdown between Pusher and our two heroes. The performances are excellent across the board, giving the sense that the actors appreciate the quality of this script.

Following a promising start with 'The Walk,' John Shiban's script for **Teso Dos Bichos** proves to be a crushing disappointment. This episode was apparently a nightmare to film (perhaps contributing to some of the overwrought supporting performances), but Kim Manners and the production crew toil admirably to inject some scares into what is a painfully weak story about ancient curses and killer cats.

Hell Money is one of those rare stories involving no paranormal phenomena whatsoever. There is still enough weirdness to keep your interest, with vanishing masked figures and frogs leaping out of corpses. However, at times, the episode's treatment of Chinese culture seems a little offensive. The most egregious example of this comes midway through the story when (for reasons that are never made clear to the audience) Mulder and Scully confront Chow, suspicious of his motives. Of course, the *point* is to make the agents look like outsiders dealing with a culture they can't understand, but the fact that their suspicions are eventually proven correct just adds insult to injury. It's hard to get excited when the story actively sets out to make the agents bystanders, observing events from afar.

For me, there is little doubt that **Jose Chung's** *From Outer Space* is Darin Morgan's finest episode. The story of Air Force personnel masquerading as 'aliens,' then being abducted by real-life aliens from 'inner space,' is at once hilarious and incredibly complex. This is one episode that benefits immensely from repeated viewings. Every scene in this entry is a character moment – telling us a bit about the participants themselves, but even more about the narrators. It's an extremely dense script that's gloriously realised and, unlike some of the show's other attempts at comedy, it is genuinely funny. A few highlights include the opening shot, the character of Blaine, and Mulder's over the top squeal.

When Skinner is suspected of murder in **Avatar**, Scully points out that he begins acting incredibly guilty. Increasing the focus on Skinner is an excellent idea and Mitch Pileggi delivers a typically strong performance, but this story suffers from trying so hard to maintain the character's ambiguity. By the end of this episode, it feels like we have learned remarkably little about Mulder and Scully's superior that we didn't already know. The character of Sharon Skinner is a welcome addition and it's a shame that there wasn't a greater focus on this relationship, given how unnecessary the attempts to connect this story to the mythology feel.

After some more experimental stories recently, **Quagmire** is a welcome return to the 'monster of the week' format. Much of the dialogue impresses, but there are also some gaping plot holes in this episode. Whether the alligator or the lake monster was responsible for the deaths (it is never made clear), the rate of attacks just happens to increase dramatically as soon as Mulder and Scully arrive. As a result, the story feels like a collection of characters simply lining up to become fish food. Regardless, it's difficult to complain when it's produced with as much flair as this.

Wetwired was scripted by the series' digital effects maestro, Mat Beck, so it's no surprise that the hallucination effects are a visual triumph. Just as impressive though is the story. The connections to the mythology feel organic here, rather than something that's been tacked on as an afterthought. It's also a testament to Gillian Anderson's performance that we actually *believe* for a moment that Scully may actually have gone off the deep end. It's a shame that the final act meanders a bit after Scully's recovery, but the brilliantly ominous meeting between the Cigarette Smoking Man and X that closes the episode is a highlight.

As an end of season cliffhanger, **Talitha Cumi** proves to be a damp squib. The opening siege is interesting in that it doesn't resemble a mythology episode at all, but the religious parallels seem oddly out of place. By the time we get to the Brothers Karamazov inspired sequences between CSM and Jeremiah Smith, it's easy to lose track of exactly what's going on. The dialogue is all very portentous and grim, but in the fullness of time this episode seems like a letdown. It adds very little to the conspiracy storyline, and imperilling a member of Mulder or Scully's family yet again this season starts to resemble a soap opera.

The third season is arguably the series' best overall. At this point, the impressive scale of the mythology episodes could still throw up tantalising clues suggestive of a larger narrative, without appearing as if the writers were simply making it up as they went along. On the standalone front, the quality of the episodes was consistently high, with Darin Morgan and Vince Gilligan contributing some of the standout stories.

The increasing popularity of the show this season clearly contributed to an increased budget that was put to good effect. It's amazing to consider that season two's 'End Game' concluded with a submarine bound set-piece in the Arctic, while this season deep-sea divers discovering aliens at the bottom of the Pacific is just a routine opening teaser. Whether it's the smoke-filled offices of the Syndicate, the black oil swimming across characters' eyes, or the agents coming across rows and rows of files in secret government facilities, some of the images from this season would justifiably go on to define the series for many viewers.

Though his few contributions to the show are widely celebrated, Darin Morgan elected not to continue with *The X-Files* after the third season (his return has been confirmed for the 2016 revival). John Shiban also joined the writing stable this year, and would remain with the show until its conclusion. As for the production crew, the establishment of the series' visual style owes a lot to the contribution of veteran director David Nutter, who joined in the series' first year and departed this season. The series' other regular directors, Rob Bowman and Kim Manners would continue to do an admirable job of crafting the show's visuals for years to come.

SEASON FOUR

The opening timber mill chase of **Herrenvolk** gets the fourth season off to a rollicking start. This scene remains the best use of the alien bounty hunter throughout the series, with the menacing and unstoppable character finally allowed to do something more than just morph and glare. The scenes of young Samantha clones are appropriately chilling and the bees offer some mystery, but like its predecessor the narrative contortions overwhelm this episode. For all the promises of big revelations, very little of any substance is actually revealed. By the time the Cigarette Smoking Man starts talking about how important Mulder is to the conspiracy's plans, you get the distinct impression that Carter has no idea where all of this is going.

The notion of 'thought photography' in **Unruhe** is an interesting premise (and one we are unlikely to see again in today's digital age). Pruitt Taylor Vince is unsettling as the main antagonist, and the serial killer storyline provides a few decent scares. In the end though, a few plot elements seem far too coincidental (particularly the six gravestones), and placing Scully in jeopardy in the final act feels too familiar. Its got potential, but some deficiencies prevent this entry from scaling any great heights.

As the most straightforward horror story that the series will ever attempt, **Home** is an exercise in narrative efficiency. When all is said and done, Mulder and Scully basically identify the killers in the first few moments, before the Sherriff is murdered and the agents storm the Peacock house. Little else happens, but the dialogue and direction are so spot-on that you barely notice. This notorious episode is not exactly subtle, but for a story that consciously sets out to disturb the audience, it certainly succeeds.

While '2Shy' took the idea behind 'Squeeze' and put a mildly interesting spin on it, **Teliko** just feels like the series cannibalising itself. The story of black men being killed by draining the pigmentation from their skin only haphazardly attempts to examine more substantial themes of racial politics. Similarly, when the identity of the killer has already been established in the teaser, it's frustrating to have Scully continually insist that the agents are investigating a public health issue. Some good jump scares in the finale unfortunately can't hide the weaknesses of the central story.

The Field Where I Died is beautifully shot, but the script is full of one too many verbose monologues. The extreme close-ups and long takes are certainly a bold approach to this material (and the actors give it their best), but the idea of the central characters being reincarnated from Civil War soldiers and holocaust victims seems heavy-handed. While this story's themes of mass suicide and doomsday cults were timely when it was first broadcast, Glen Morgan & James Wong's contributions to *Millennium* dealt with the Book of Revelations and the associated religious imagery in a far more satisfying way.

And people thought 'Home' was gory! **Sanguinarium** piles on the blood in a blur of scalpels and pentagram motifs. The premise of a hopelessly vain plastic surgeon is ripe for satire but, in the best traditions of 'so-so' *X-Files*, Mulder and Scully just aren't given enough to do here. Some of the imagery is brutal, but at times this feels like the leads are simply guiding the audience through proceedings instead of playing an active part.

The first real flashback episode, **Musings of a Cigarette Smoking Man** is a mostly effective examination of the series' central antagonist. The early scenes depicting CSM as the assassin of JFK and Martin Luther King are by far the best. Bizarrely, the character's trivial everyday concerns in the final act end up seeming more far-fetched than the conspiracy claptrap we have just witnessed. William B. Davis does what he can with the scenes depicting CSM as a frustrated writer, but this material is just too far removed from the character we have come to know (and of course, that's the point). It's unclear whether any of this is canon, but most casual viewers apparently accept this episode's 'musings' as the true history of the character.

Aside from **Paper Hearts**, no other episode successfully manages to have the audience question the accepted wisdom of Samantha Mulder's disappearance. This is partly a result of the excellent script, but it also owes a lot to the talents of Tom Noonan. His performance helps to place John Lee Roche among the scariest (and most human) monsters the series has ever presented. Special mention should also go to the elegantly simple, but effective, dream sequences. A fourth season highlight.

After examining the Second World War's Axis powers in season three, the fourth season turns its attention to the Cold War in **Tunguska** and **Terma**. The former is a mostly effective set up, reintroducing the black oil and Krycek. Scully investigates the black oil carrying meteorite while Mulder ventures to Russia. The use of the flashforward device in the teaser, an *X-Files* staple, has probably never been more bewildering than it is in 'Tunguska.' As exciting as the Russia-set sequences are, in 'Terma' the writers have to acknowledge how confusing events have become. Their solution is for characters to deliver long mouthfuls of expository dialogue reminding us how we got here. As a result, Scully's testimony before a Senate committee is completely devoid of tension or drama. The oil-well climax injects some much-needed action, but the promise of the first episode feels like it's been wasted.

El Mundo Gira and **Kaddish** are two more stories told through the lenses of different cultures. Neither episode scales any great heights, but they approach their subject matter in very different ways. In examining the Mexican myth of the chupacabra, 'El Mundo Gira' frames the story as a melodramatic soap opera. The metaphors and performances may not be subtle, but for the most part it works. Ruben Blades is fun as the INS agent, and the fungal effects are excellent. Unfortunately, Vancouver doesn't resemble southern California at all, making this one of the few scripts that would have benefited from being produced a few seasons later. 'Kaddish,' meanwhile, plays it deadly serious. The only thing grimmer than this entry's atmosphere is its characters. The cultural issues are handled much more sensitively and genuinely than other similar stories, and Mark Snow's score is a particular highlight. Ultimately though, the golem storyline of a monster run amok just seems a bit too familiar.

As Glen Morgan & James Wong's final episode, **Never Again** feels just as unorthodox as their other fourth season entries. As with '3,' you have to appreciate their gall in having one of the leads jump into bed with a minor secondary character (and a violent psycho, nonetheless). The writers were apparently disappointed that the original scheduling of this episode implied that Scully's behaviour was motivated by an awareness of her cancer. Such issues aside, the character feels so different here from the rest of the series that it's difficult for the viewer to connect with Scully at all. Everything feels very grungy and gritty, and it's perhaps because of this that this entry barely resembles an *X-File* at all.

With **Leonard Betts**, the series once again revisits the idea of a mutant who feeds off human tissue to survive – this time it's tumors (sometimes you suspect they're just listing body parts for these creatures in the writer's room...) What distinguishes this from previous storylines is the playful tone and the sympathetic character of Leonard. By the time he gives birth to a new body it's in danger of getting a little too ridiculous, but the script manages to straddle the line between sincerity and pastiche well in the final scenes. This may be the highest-rating episode in the history of the series, but most people could easily name several better entries. Still, the final scene remains an ingenious way of leaving the audience on tenterhooks.

Scully's cancer is introduced in **Memento Mori**, and the episode does a pretty good job of bringing together various threads of the mythology in a briskly paced affair. Some of the narration is a bit longwinded, but it's good to see Mulder teaming up with the Lone Gunmen to get them out in the field for a change. Skinner's deal with the devil to save Scully also proves a very tantalising prospect. At the time, this episode felt incredibly consequential. In hindsight though, Gillian Anderson appears underserviced by a story that should see her character take centre stage.

Unrequited rarely comes up in any discussion of the series' classics, but for the most part it's an extremely worthwhile standalone episode. The sequence in the Pentagon is as tense and effective as anything the series has produced before or since. The episode also has something interesting to say about American society's problems in dealing with the at times 'invisible' veterans of Vietnam, and for that reason it's only natural that Skinner gets an expanded role. Unfortunately, the teaser (where we flashforward to the climax) lowers the stakes considerably in the final scenes.

Tempus Fugit and **Max** are ostensibly part of the mythology, but in truth we learn nothing new of substance over the course of this two-parter. This is really a series of events strung together around a single set-piece. It's an admittedly impressive set-piece, and it's hard to complain when the production is executed as well as it is here. 'Tempus Fugit' opens proceedings well, with an interesting teaser and a fantastic supporting performance from Joe Spano. It hits the action beats too, especially the excellent runway chase sequence. Unfortunately, 'Max' isn't able to maintain quite the same degree of momentum. The acting and direction are both strong, but the story feels a little like it's on auto-pilot when the agents are given access to alien technology simply by collecting Max's mail (something they probably should have done earlier) and the climax is essentially just a repeat of the previous episode's opening teaser. Still, for an exercise built around a special-effects rig, it's very enjoyable and stands out as one of the series' more successful two-part stories.

The concept of time-travel is approached in a very *X-Files* way in **Synchrony**. The freezing effects are very good, and there are some fun moments, but the characters all feel a little underdeveloped. It's perfectly watchable, but you may struggle to recall much about the story afterwards.

Small Potatoes starts with a cute mystery of a small town where babies are being born with tails. Pretty soon, the father is revealed to be the shape-changing character of Eddie Van Blundht (played by former writer Darin Morgan). The explanation for Eddie's morphing ability is dealt with in a throwaway line of dialogue, because Vince Gilligan's script is really just asking the question, what would an ordinary person think of Mulder and Scully's lifestyles? As you'd expect, the script is clever and incisive. 'Small Potatoes' is wish fulfilment of the basest kind, but watching it is so much damn fun that you barely notice.

For some reason, **Zero Sum** seems to get a lot of hate amongst fans. While the substance of the story may have little influence on the rest of the mythology, it is encouraging to see the series quickly acknowledging events that have gone before. Skinner's reluctant deal with the Cigarette Smoking Man could so easily have become another mythology non-sequitur, but this episode works well as a direct sequel to 'Memento Mori.' While Scully may be absent and Mulder's presence is dramatically reduced, Mitch Pileggi more than holds his own. The plot feels a little circuitous but, as far as Skinner episodes are concerned, any story that ends with him emptying a clip in CSM's direction is pretty satisfying.

Ostensibly about messages sent from the dead to the dying, **Elegy** is another episode that expressly deals with Scully's cancer. The haunting visuals are excellent, and the supporting performances endearing. When you look back at the series as a whole, the storyline of Scully's cancer loses a great deal of significance (the whole device is introduced and wrapped up within a dozen or so episodes). Perhaps it could have been more resonant if the writers had given us more standalone storylines dealing with themes of mortality as they do here, rather than poring over the ongoing machinations of the conspiracy.

Like 'Paper Hearts,' **Demons** attempts to recast the mystery of Samantha's abduction, this time as a domestic dispute. It's a fun idea (given what we have learned about the Mulder family so far) but with the benefit of hindsight it really doesn't reveal much at all. That's not the fault of R.W. Goodwin, who impresses in his one and only scripting assignment. It's just that there's only so many times we can revisit the Samantha storyline without being provided with some definitive answers. The flashback sequences are masterfully handled by director Kim Manners.

The epic scale of **Gethsemane** is its biggest asset – sweeping shots of Canadian peaks accompanied by Mark Snow's fantastic score still manage to impress. As for the story, the possibility that Mulder may *finally* hold definitive proof of alien life genuinely tantalises for a moment. But the weakness of this script lies in the credibility of its cliffhanger. Having seen Mulder come close to the truth only to have it snatched away so many times before, it beggars belief that he would now be so wracked by self-doubt as to commit suicide (telling the story in flashback only amplifies this deficiency). Still, you can't take anything away from the production crew when they're able to deliver images as startling as this at the end of a gruelling schedule.

There is some debate over which of the fourth or fifth seasons is *The X-Files'* most popular – in terms of raw viewer numbers, the fifth season achieved slightly better average ratings – however a strong argument can be made that the fourth season was the zenith of the show's popularity. The quality of the show's stand-alone episodes this year remained high, although not as consistently impressive as the previous season. Given that Chris Carter and Frank Spotnitz 'broke' the story for the first movie after the third season, we also know that there was a definitive plan for where the mythology was headed this year (perhaps for the first time). The fourth season largely benefits from this certainty, with a strong mix of one-off and two-part mythology episodes.

Three writers who had been with the series from the beginning, Glen Morgan & James Wong, as well as Howard Gordon, departed for the final time this season. Along with Chris Carter, each of these creative talents made significant contributions to the establishment of the show's signature style, but series regulars like Frank Spotnitz, John Shiban and Vince Gilligan would continue to put their imprint on the show until the final season.

SEASON FIVE

Like so many middle instalments of three-part episodes, you can't escape the feeling that **Redux** is stalling for time. The episode groans under the weight of its endless narration, even though John Finn's delivery of Kritschgau's Cold War monologue is a highlight. While the images of Mulder deep within the labyrinthine tunnels of the Pentagon are impressive, there is no real cliffhanger to speak of and by the conclusion the narrative has only barely progressed.

The events of **Redux II** carry a lot more weight than those of its predecessor, largely because these events *finally* catch up to the present-day and we can dispense with the superfluous narration. Mulder's interactions with the Cigarette Smoking Man are fun, even if no one believes that really is Samantha. The final scene montage of Mulder giving evidence, while Scully is given the last rites and the Cigarette Smoking Man is gunned down, feels appropriately momentous. The only disappointment with this entry is where it leaves the characters – 'Redux II' kicks off the season-long arc of Mulder reassessing his own beliefs, but this whole storyline just gives the appearance of the series navel-gazing in anticipation of the movie.

At this point in the series, an episode devoted almost entirely to the Lone Gunmen seems like an appealing prospect. Fortunately, **Unusual Suspects** delivers on this promise. The 'prequel' aspect of this episode is its greatest asset. Seeing the trio meet for the first time (along with appearances from a young Mulder and X) gives this material extra weight. Lone Gunmen stories set in the present (including their spin-off series) will somehow never feel as substantial as this. Mulder's exposure to a paranoia inducing chemical here also dovetails nicely into this season's arc about his possibly misplaced belief in extraterrestrials.

Detour is a fifth season standalone favourite. Continuing the tradition of 'Ice' and 'Darkness Falls,' this instalment finds the agents being pursued by invisible creatures while isolated in the Florida wilderness. It's an effective set up, and the visuals once again owe a great debt to Vancouver's lush forests. The agents building a tower of corpses in the climax (echoing Mulder's earlier disgust at 'team building' exercises), is one of those moments that only *The X-Files* could pull off. Unfortunately, it's let down by the unnecessary revelations about the creatures' origin in the final act.

The Post-Modern Prometheus is the first episode written and directed by Chris Carter since season three. It's a fun ride for the most part, but perhaps not quite as fun as it thinks it is. The performances of Chris Owens and John O'Hurley are enjoyable, and the black and white photography certainly looks great. It's possible to cope with the central monster, the 'circus' tent motif, and even Cher, but the episode overdoes it a little with the quirky townspeople, especially as this type of thing was done far more successfully in 'Humbug.' The final scene is rightly celebrated as a great 'shipper' moment, but it's worth emphasising that the series still consigns such events to fantasy at this stage.

The series' first real yuletide entry, **Christmas Carol** feels about as far removed from a mythology episode as you can get. It's an interesting experiment to focus almost entirely on Scully's family (Mulder's two-second appearance is very strange, and frankly a bit unnecessary). Some strong performances are on offer, including John Pyper Ferguson as the detective, but this experiment only partly succeeds. Mythology episodes work best when information is revealed with a sense of urgency – by interspersing quaint flashbacks to Scully's early life, this episode verges dangerously close to sappy melodrama. It's a shame that the writers don't even attempt to explain the mysterious phone calls, but the final scene revelation is a great twist.

The change of tone between 'Christmas Carol' and **Emily** is a little jarring. Perhaps afraid that the previous episode treaded too lightly, the writers notably ratchet up the conspiracy atmosphere in this outing. Scully's biological daughter is suddenly spouting green blood and clone fertility doctors are everywhere. This feels like far more familiar territory for the series, but unfortunately it leaves little time to focus on what should be an incredibly emotional period for Scully. There are some quietly affecting scenes in the final act but, seen in context, it feels like the series managed to forget the character of Emily a bit too quickly.

Robert Modell from 'Pusher' returns in **Kitsunegari**, but unfortunately this episode never reaches the heights of its predecessor. Some of the imagery is strong, particularly the character who dies ingesting 'cerulean blue' paint. But this entry is weaker for switching the focus away from Modell to a sister character we have never seen or heard of before. Whereas the first 'Pusher' presented its narrative objectively, 'Kitsunegari' repeatedly uses the conceit of putting us in the characters' shoes, showing us their distorted version of reality. It's a noble attempt, but the series will go on to achieve this effect better in later episodes.

Schizogeny examines some pretty dark themes of abuse breeding abuse, and the familiar storyline of teenage angst is actually one of this episode's strongest features. Unfortunately though, the guilty party is telegraphed very early on, and once we know who is responsible the 'killer roots' motif starts to get a little ridiculous...even for this show.

Stephen King's contributions to **Chinga** were reportedly extensively rewritten by Chris Carter. This results in a wildly shifting tone (particularly in the Mulder scenes) that makes the episode a difficult one to love. As you would expect from King, it contains some frightening scares, but these moments seem to owe a greater debt to the talents of director Kim Manners than the script.

While 'Chinga' displays signs of a guest writer struggling with the series' characters, **Kill Switch** shares none of these problems. The central narrative of uploading a human consciousness on to the internet sounds very far-fetched, but it manages to retain some credibility by being handled in a particularly *X-Files* way. It's good to see the Lone Gunmen given something to do, and William Gibson and Tom Maddox certainly seem to enjoy writing for the geeky trio. Rob Bowman's cinematic direction is able to show off the series' increasing budget, with plenty of explosions and shootouts on offer in this fun entry.

A fan favourite, **Bad Blood** manages to skewer many of the series' conventions in a way that is more reverent and affectionate than Darin Morgan's episodes. The actors clearly relish the opportunity to play around with their characters, and Luke Wilson gives a good supporting performance. It's great for fans, but some of the jokes are so meta – like when Mulder corrects Scully on the name of the hotel as the location crawls across the bottom of the screen – you wonder what a first-time viewer would make of it all. An audience's enjoyment of 'Bad Blood' seems to depend largely on one's familiarity with the tropes of the series.

Although still set in the real world, in **Patient X** and **The Red & The Black** the series' mythology becomes even bolder and more elaborate. Given the sometimes shocking images that the mythology has given us over the years, it's telling that these episodes contain some of the series' most brutal (Dmitri's sewn up mouths and eyelids are particularly gruesome). It's good to see Krycek and Marita Covarrubias back, as well as Brian Thompson's bounty hunter. The introductions of Jeffrey and Cassandra Spender are less satisfying – if only because the arc of these characters should have been so much more tragic. Likewise, the season-long arc of Mulder and Scully reversing their traditional sceptic/believer roles is wrapped up in record-time. Despite this, the episodes feel very epic. It's a shame that this sense of scale is undercut by the conclusion which, like most mythology episodes, shirks at offering any satisfying resolution.

When discussing people's favourite episodes, **Travelers** rarely rates a mention. Though perhaps understandable given that Scully is absent (and Mulder barely appears), it's a shame because it serves as an excellent period piece. The costuming, production design and even the cinematography do a great job of establishing the era. The script's focus on 1950s Cold War paranoia and the "Red menace" also dovetails nicely with the mythology's recent forays into Russian gulags and arms races. Overall, it's a diversion, but an admirable one.

Mind's Eye is a pretty dull entry. The concept of a blind woman seeing through the eyes of a killer is an interesting premise, and it's assisted by some strong supporting performances, but the tone is so overwhelmingly grim that this one can be a pretty tough slog to sit through.

All Souls continues the series' examination of religion, but adopts a quite different tone to its predecessors. But for the presence of the leads, this feels much more akin to an episode of *Millennium*. Mulder's readiness to believe in almost anything, with the notable exception of religious phenomena in episodes like this, might work better if he wasn't so achingly unsympathetic to his partner's perspective. It is also interesting to see the series (briefly) acknowledge the character of Emily.

By far John Shiban's best contribution to the series, **The Pine Bluff Variant** is a tour-de-force from start to finish. It's difficult to make an audience question a central character's allegiances at this point in the series, but by juxtaposing Mulder's own distrust of the government with a fanatical militia, the script manages to do just that. Some great supporting performances and stunning examples of Vancouver's locations are on display here. The bio-weapon macguffin also feels very ahead of its time. One of the highlights of the fifth season, this episode feels as cinematic as anything the series has produced before or since.

Folie à Deux kicks off with high-drama, and the scenes of a siege in a call centre are certainly very well done. The tone then shifts, as Mulder suspects that the gunman may not have been as crazy as he seemed. Despite the monster apparently looking laughable on the set, the video and post-production effects used to conceal the costume are very effective, simply adding to the uncertainty about whether or not this thing is real or a figment of someone's imagination. It's fun to see Mulder (finally) end up in restraints, and Vince Gilligan's script is typically witty.

With **The End**, the series concludes the process of setting up the first feature film that started at the beginning of season four. The Cigarette Smoking Man's return surprises no one (it's worth questioning whether his 'death' at the start of this season was necessary at all). Despite this, it's a strong mythology episode that manages to pack plenty in to its brief running time. The reassignment of Mulder and Scully feels almost familiar by now, but the image of the x-files office in flames proves quite powerful. The introduction of Gibson Praise and Diana Fowley is handled pretty well, even if the arcs of these characters will ultimately prove unsatisfying. It's also good to see Vancouver finally playing itself, having added so much to the series' first five seasons.

While some of the fifth season's stories are hit-and-miss, the overall quality of the episodes remains high. This unusually short season represents a watershed moment in the evolution of *The X-Files*. It was the last to be filmed in Vancouver, and serves primarily as a precursor to the first feature film. Having gone into production after the feature film (but *before* its release), it is easy to get the sense that the mythology has been treading water a little this year. In hindsight, some of the storylines feel perfunctory; like Mulder reassessing his belief in extraterrestrials, or Scully's all too brief relationship with Emily. In both cases these attempts at drama were wrapped up far too quickly, never to be heard from again. That being said, the introduction of a rebel alien race would prove substantive in the following season.

The upheaval caused by the show's relocation to Los Angeles meant the loss of numerous crew members who had helped to shape the tone of the series from the beginning. Chief among the production crew lost this season was the series' Executive Producer overseeing production in Vancouver, R.W. Goodwin. It is to Chris Carter and the rest of the producers' credit that the crew assembled in Los Angeles was equally strong. Those crew members would go on to do a fine job forging a new identity for the series, albeit without the abundant atmosphere of Vancouver. Plenty of people maintain that the series could have ended here, and while consistency certainly became an issue in the later years of The X-Files, it would still be a shame to miss out on some of the excellent episodes that follow.

FIGHT THE FUTURE

The first *X-Files* feature film, **Fight the Future**, is occasionally criticised for too closely resembling the television show. I have never really understood these criticisms, given that the film *must* resemble the series in order to maintain a semblance of continuity, while simultaneously offering something new. It's true that Chris Carter and Frank Spotnitz's story could probably have been told on the television series' smaller canvas, but the smaller budget and scheduling constraints would undoubtedly have required compromises. Film being primarily a visual medium, the epic scale of the imagery on display here is impressive, and ultimately serves as a welcome addition to *The X-Files* canon.

Rob Bowman's self-assured direction showcases wonderful visuals that the television series could only dream of – prehistoric flashbacks, exploding buildings, and a jaw-dropping final act set in Antarctica. As you would expect, the special effects are excellent, making good use of the cinema's broader frame. What's most impressive about this entry is the sense of grandeur, with Mark Snow's fully orchestral score making a significant contribution in this regard.

Gillian Anderson and David Duchovny deliver confident performances, although it must be said that this material doesn't really stretch them (Scully's flirtation with quitting the bureau seems to last barely a scene). It's notable that despite being shot primarily in Los Angeles, the crew did travel to Canada to capture some of the cold-weather sequences. In doing so, the film manages to retain the series' trademark atmosphere, no doubt assisted by the fact that the director was one of the main parties responsible for establishing the 'look' of the television show.

The story deserves praise for adding something new to the mythology, while still remaining comprehensible for a wide audience. Some apparently believe the film underserved the mythology – as it is though, the narrative manages to coherently pull together five years of arcs, with appearances from all the major players. It's true that Krycek is absent, and there is precious little mention of Samantha (at least in the theatrical version), but you can understand why the decision was made to excise such elements. Not every mythology episode includes explicit references to Samantha, or Krycek, or Scully's abduction, and nor should they. The filmmakers have only two hours in which to service a concise narrative, without overstuffing it full of arbitrary references merely for fan-service.

The movie is certainly not perfect, just barely managing to serve as a bridge between the fifth and sixth seasons. Indeed, it's one of the few films based on a television series to be released while the show was still on the air. Despite this (or maybe because of it), 'Fight the Future' is best viewed in isolation. As a summer blockbuster, and as an opportunity to see the series finally deliver on its claims of being cinematic, it works very well.

SEASON SIX

Appropriately, **The Beginning** opens with a shot of the sun beating down over a harsh desert. The series directly addresses its relocation to Los Angeles and announces that it will be making the most of its new filming environment. The action-packed narrative (it's basically one long extended chase sequence) manages to satisfactorily wrap up the combined events of 'The End' and 'Fight the Future.' It is disappointing though that none of the last three entries manages to achieve an entirely consistent feel, but this was probably inevitable given the changes in production crews and shooting locations. Taken on its own, 'The Beginning' is a tentatively promising start to the next stage of *The X-Files*.

Vince Gilligan's script for **Drive** is an incredibly taught piece, containing more conspiracy and sci-fi elements than any of his other solo efforts since 'Soft Light.' Bryan Cranston shines as Crump, and it's a good thing too because this episode could have easily fallen flat without such a nuanced supporting performance. It's also good to see Scully given something to do here – the scene of her investigating the trailer park is wonderfully eerie. The tension throughout this entry is palpable, making the ending all the more tragic.

Like last season's 'The Post-Modern Prometheus,' **Triangle** is Chris Carter's attempt at something different. The pace is so fast and all elements of the production so polished – from the costuming, to the score, to the editing – that it is hard not to get swept away. The story may at times resemble a comic-book, but in terms of sheer entertainment value, 'Triangle' is an unqualified success.

It's a struggle to think of a two-parter that is less consequential than **Dreamland** and **Dreamland II**, but few have as much fun with their premise as these episodes. The body-switching story-line ostensibly resembles 'Small Potatoes,' but the difference here is that we also get to see Mulder struggle with his alternate life as a domesticated Man In Black. It's a fun idea, and it's good to see the series making full use of its new location by setting a story within Area 51. However the decision to stretch this story across *two* episodes seems like a mistake – it gives the writers plenty of opportunity for gags, but after a while (and particularly by the second instalment) it just feels like the same joke being repeated again and again. Michael McKean gives an accomplished comedic performance, but by the time this concludes and time snaps back, you might be left wondering what the point of it all was.

How the Ghosts Stole Christmas starts promisingly, with the prospect of a spooky ghost story, but it quickly descends into a quirky character study. This wouldn't normally be a bad thing, but 'Dreamland' and 'Dreamland II' covered very similar ground, and many other episodes this season will do the same. It's also nowhere near as funny as it thinks it is… The production design is magnificent, and Ed Asner and Lily Tomlin deliver strong supporting performances, but I just wish Chris Carter had stuck to his guns and delivered the genuinely creepy haunted house story that this could have been.

Terms of Endearment is about as close to horror as the sixth season gets, but it's telling that this entry still plays its subject matter very lightly. The scene of Spender casually shredding the report (before Mulder digs it out of the garbage) is fun, and Bruce

Campbell is good as the demon who just wants a normal child. The plot puts a surprising spin on the concept, but once the twist is revealed the episode offers little else to keep the audience interested.

Romantic comedy is not a genre people would normally associate with *The X-Files*. That being said, **The Rain King** makes a solid attempt at this sort of material. As with most of the stories this season, the script wastes little time offering credible scientific explanations and instead jumps straight into various scenes of wacky-weather related phenomena. These inventive scenarios, like heart-shaped hail and cow-tossing tornadoes, are the best parts of the episode. The supporting cast go a bit over the top with their performances, and the sappy tone of the episode can become a little grating by the end, but the series now has enough self-awareness for the characters to actually point this out.

Like 'The Pine Bluff Variant,' **S.R. 819** is another strong one-off conspiracy episode from John Shiban. The nanotechnology storyline is well handled, and it's always a pleasure to see Mitch Pileggi get more screen-time. The effects are mostly excellent, and the ominous ending allows the character of Skinner (whose motivations really should be clear-cut by now) to retain a hint of menace. Once again though, the flash-forward to the final scene (a device that the series uses repeatedly) is not entirely successful here.

Tithonus is a sixth season gem, dealing with its central theme of mortality in an intelligent, yet emotionally powerful way. New series producer Michael Watkins directs the script with flair, and the black-and-white colourisation effects are impressive. Special mention should also go to the late Geoffrey Lewis for his world-weary performance as Fellig. This is one of those occasions where splitting up the central characters doesn't feel forced, and it's also one of the few times this season where the series manages to convincingly depict somewhere other than southern California.

Trumpeted as the 'end of the conspiracy,' **Two Fathers** and **One Son** feel heftier than most mythology episodes (and having the Cigarette Smoking Man narrate the history of the conspiracy certainly adds to this air of self-importance). It's a bit difficult to understand how Cassandra Spender is the 'first' alien/human hybrid given that we've apparently seen several already (The Erlenmeyer Flask, 731, Memento Mori, Emily), but the events of the first episode move along briskly enough that it doesn't really matter. The final destruction of the Syndicate happening off-screen proves to be a bit of an anti-climax, but we should be used to that sort of thing with the mythology by now. It's also no accident that key players manage to survive these events, somewhat undermining the purpose of the episodes. This also 'feels' different from other mythology entries – the lighting, and even the film stock, seem so far removed from previous episodes that it can become distracting. Overall though, it's an appropriate time to relaunch the series' ongoing arc and Carter and Spotnitz do an admirable job of wrapping up six years of storylines.

In **Agua Mala**, the production manages to simulate a pretty convincing hurricane, but the biggest weakness of this entry is the tone. We have seen before that isolating Mulder and Scully can produce real tension, but David Amann's script persists with the same light-hearted tone that permeates the rest of this season. When the characters on-screen seem so untroubled by people disappearing around them, it's hard for the audience to be too concerned about their fate.

In presenting essentially the same series of events over and over again, **Monday** has a difficult job. It mostly succeeds because Kim Manners shoots it interestingly enough that each individual sequence offers something new, despite the familiarity. The bank explosion is brilliantly realised, but the success of this story really depends on the sincerity of the supporting cast. To Carrie Hamilton's credit, she delivers a great performance as the tortured woman endlessly reliving the same day.

Arcadia and **Alpha** are two very different examples of standalone episodes by new writers to the show. Daniel Arkin's 'Arcadia' relies on the gimmick of Mulder and Scully going undercover as a married couple, and has become something of a fan favourite. The story of a gated community with something to hide manages to strike a balance between the manicured lawns on display, and the seamy underbelly that's hidden from view. The script isn't overly ambitious, but it's one of those rare episodes that actually benefits from the picturesque surrounds of southern California. Jeffrey Bell's 'Alpha,' on the other hand, is a crushing disappointment. Essentially a werewolf story set in the city, it's neither witty, nor scary. The production crew tries to inject a creepy atmosphere into proceedings, but it ends up being a very by-the-numbers entry.

Trevor takes the fairly simple premise of a man who can walk through walls and manages to fashion it into an entertaining hour of television. The return to the series' signature dark atmosphere is welcome, with this entry dropping the lighter tone that has pervaded much of this season. The story is merely solid, but there are some memorable visuals and the special effects are excellent.

Milagro proves that there is still something to be learned about the lead characters after all these years. John Hawkes delivers a great performance as the writer who imagines characters so perfectly that they come to life. Chris Carter's script includes some florid and occasionally incomprehensible narration, but thankfully it doesn't overwhelm the main plot. Indeed, the murder sequences are some of the scariest that the series has depicted in a long time.

The Unnatural brings some genuine emotion to its cartoony premise of an alien baseball star, with the balance between wackiness and pathos perfectly fitting the tone of this season. The period sequences are beautifully realised, and in his directorial debut Duchovny shrewdly directs the actors in these scenes to mostly play it straight. On the other hand, the Mulder and Scully scenes that bookend the episode are cute, even if both actors' performances are a tad goofier than normal. A fine debut entry.

While 'Unusual Suspects' exemplified the potential of *The Lone Gunmen* spin-off series, **Three of a Kind** glaringly displays that concept's limitations. With Mulder absent, Scully and the geeky trio hit Vegas... and that's about it. It's a stop-gap episode to pass the time, but one where very little of substance occurs. Like many episodes of the spin-off series that will follow, any threat to the protagonists is completely undercut by the endlessly quirky tone.

A sixth season highlight, **Field Trip** is an alternate reality tale with so many twists and turns that it leaves the audience's head spinning in the best possible way. Episodes like 'Bad Blood' and 'Kill Switch' hinted at this kind of thing, but it's exhilarating to see the series embrace the concept so boldly here. While the broader story examines Mulder and Scully's perception of each another, the final frames also serve to keep the audience questioning the nature of our own reality long after the credits have rolled.

As an attempt to reinvent the mythology for a post-Syndicate era, **Biogenesis** proves to be merely adequate. We get many of the same players like the Cigarette Smoking Man, Fowley and Krycek, but the presence of these characters occasionally just feels superfluous to the plot (even if there is a welcome acknowledgement of the events of 'S.R. 819'). The attempts to connect the mythology to a broader examination of religion are interesting, as is the image of Scully standing before a UFO, but it's a shame that this cliffhanger will prove to be a letdown in subsequent episodes.

There's no denying that most of this season's episodes have a very different feel to those that came before. This can only partly be explained by the series' relocation to Los Angeles, with many of the scripts actively embracing a more humorous tone. You certainly can't accuse the series' formula of going stale at this point, but for the first time in several years inconsistency in the quality of individual episodes became apparent this season. It is interesting to see the series try something different, but ultimately *The X-Files* is not a comedy series and even if many of this season's entries may be amusing, few are laugh-out-loud funny.

By this stage, the show had become so entrenched in popular culture that some degree of self-parody was probably inevitable. While season six's ratings dipped from the previous year, they still remained relatively strong. Finally resolving the mythology in 'Two Fathers' and 'One Son' was a shrewd move, with the complex backstory and constantly shifting allegiances in danger of overwhelming even the most die-hard viewers. Despite what some will say, the series' later mythology episodes do have their moments, even if the character of the Cigarette Smoking Man is somewhat neutered from this season onwards.

New writers to the show this season included David Amann, Jeffrey Bell and Daniel Arkin. Ken Hawryliw, the series' former props master and cameo player in 'Unusual Suspects,' also contributed the script for 'Trevor' with Jim Guttridge this year. Michael Watkins joined the series' producing and directing ranks, while Bryan Spicer would go on to make a significant contribution to *The Lone Gunmen* spin-off series. Daniel Sackheim, who had served as a producer on the pilot and the movie, also contributed the last of his four episodes this season.

SEASON SEVEN

It's very hard to escape the conclusion that the narrative of **The Sixth Extinction** is biding time. At the start of *The X-Files'* seventh season, Mulder is in hospital suffering from brain abnormalities and Scully is standing in front of a UFO on a beach in West Africa. By the end of this episode, Scully has returned but little else has changed. The return of Kritschgau proves unexpected, but you almost *wish* that Mulder had written Krycek's name instead to invest these expository scenes with a bit more conflict. Nicholas Lea doesn't even make an appearance in this entry and, with Krycek meriting only cameos in the surrounding instalments, his character is starting to feel very underused. Where this episode does excel is in the dramatic imagery it depicts – boiling seas of blood, biblical plagues, and people rising from the dead. These visuals may not progress the story much, but their good fun to watch.

Like 'Christmas Carol' before it, **The Sixth Extinction II: Amor Fati** is that rare mythology episode that doubles as a character study. Mulder is now a Christ-like figure, operated on and brought close to death by the Cigarette Smoking Man (his father, apparently!) for reasons that are skipped over far too quickly. The bulk of the runtime is devoted to Mulder's visions; and while these contain a brief hint of the apocalyptic imagery we saw previously, his dreams consist mainly of sandcastle spaceships and domestic bliss. It's a dramatic change of pace, and the shift in tone from the earlier instalments doesn't feel natural at all. Whilst this trilogy has been a noble attempt to revive the mythology, the fact that many of these threads will be largely forgotten in future stories suggests that the experiment didn't quite succeed.

Hungry was actually the first entry of the seventh season to be filmed (you can tell because Gillian Anderson and David Duchovny appear to still be on holiday). By telling this story from the monster's perspective, Vince Gilligan tries something different. Rob Roberts proves to be a sympathetic character, but the plot just seems to meander from one scene of him reluctantly killing people to the next. Nevertheless, this unique storytelling device manages to elevate what would otherwise be another forgettable tale of a monster eating human body parts, to an episode that at least holds some interest.

For those who haven't had the pleasure, Chris Carter's *Millennium* is an at times frustrating, always unsettling, and occasionally brilliant series. It's a shame that this **Millennium** doesn't satisfactorily capture the essence of that series, because its not a particularly strong episode of *The X-Files* either. No matter how much the writers try to dress it up with religious jargon, it's a routine zombie story that hardly seems worthy of either show. Aside from the much-hyped kiss between Mulder and Scully, this entry is really only worth it to see Lance Henriksen as Frank Black reunited with his daughter once again.

The series returns to its staple subject-matter of 'angsty teens' with **Rush**. David Amann's script makes the mistake of telegraphing the killer's identity in the teaser, not for the first time rendering Mulder and Scully (along with the audience) mere observers of the action. The super-speed special effects are visually impressive, but there is little else to recommend it.

The central premise of **The Goldberg Variation** – that one man's good luck results in all those around him suffering – is an admittedly clever one. After a while though, Willie Garson's performance and the sheer ridiculousness of the real-life Rube Goldberg scenarios becomes hard to swallow. The ending of this entry is also so sappy and maudlin that it makes some of the sixth season's episodes appear sombre by comparison.

Like 'Kitsunegari,' **Orison** sees the return of one of the series' more memorable villains. But just as that fifth season episode suffered from shifting the focus to a new antagonist, this entry also neglects its central villain to devote far too much time to the secondary character of Reverend Orison. As you would expect from Rob Bowman, the slow-motion sequences are visually arresting. Some viewers take exception to Scully killing Pfaster in the finale, but my main gripe with this instalment is that it quite *literally* makes his character into the devil incarnate, thereby cheapening the wonderful ambiguity of 'Irresistible.'

With its clever use of heist-movie staples, **The Amazing Maleeni** manages to strike the right balance between quirky humour and the obligatory plot twists. The script parses out just enough information to keep you intrigued by the central mystery, instead of relying entirely on coincidence like 'The Goldberg Variation' (although there are still plenty of fluke occurrences here). The prosthetics are pretty convincing, but unfortunately the use of CGI in the opening teaser leaves a lot to be desired and only serves to undermine the final reveal.

Signs & Wonders is another episode examining religious themes, contrasting the snake-handlers of the Bible belt with more conventional worshippers. The use of real snakes results in some terrifying scenes – full credit to the production crew – but for the second episode in a row we are treated to some very shoddy CGI. The killer's reveal is genuinely unexpected (and it's good to see the series skewering organised religion), but aside from the snake scenes the rest of the episode is a tad unsatisfying.

Personally, **Sein Und Zeit** and **Closure** are two of the series' most disappointing episodes. The first entry is a pretty standard kidnapping story, with only subtle parallels to the disappearance of Mulder's own sister. When a little girl was kidnapped in 'Oubliette,' Mulder argued forcefully that his life was not entirely dictated by that single childhood experience. In this episode though, he's reduced to an emotional wreck (even before his mother's very abrupt death). The cliffhanging reveal that these children were victims of a serial killer is extremely confronting, and the atmospheric scenes around the graves are a highlight. But 'Closure' then changes tack completely, as the agents begin investigating Samantha's disappearance with the help of a psychic (something you feel they perhaps could have done earlier...) The final reveal is a genuinely emotional moment, and Kim Manners' direction is superb. But aside from a brief appearance from the Cigarette Smoking Man, these episodes don't *feel* like they fit within the rest of the mythology at all. The concept of walk-ins is frankly ridiculous, and it seems like Carter and Spotnitz straining to deliver an answer the viewer won't expect. Despite the obvious skill with which these episodes were crafted, 'Paper Hearts' remains a superior example of this storyline's potential to surprise the audience.

X-Cops is a widely renowned episode, and while the story can seem a little thin, the acclaim is deserved if only for the sheer inventiveness of the premise. True to Vince Gilligan's vision, it feels as if Mulder and Scully just happened to come across a film crew, with the production crew managing to perfectly capture the atmosphere of a typical *Cops* episode. It's not entirely satisfying as an *X-File*, but as an exercise in testing the limits of the series' format, 'X-Cops' is without equal.

Following on from the promise of 'Kill Switch,' William Gibson and Tom Maddox deliver a disappointing effort with **First Person Shooter**. The themes and implications of virtual reality are barely touched upon, as the script sees character after character simply line up to enter a deadly videogame. It's clear that the production crew is consciously playing up the juvenile nature of the game, but the overall tone feels very wrong. Chris Carter directs some-one else's script for the first time, and although the game se-quences admittedly look cool, the narrative is threadbare.

Billy Drago's performance is the best aspect of **Theef**. Some of the death scenes are gruesome, and the episode is able to generate a very creepy feel (in spite of the California setting). While the pro-duction looks great, the script was reportedly written at extremely short notice. This is evident from the weakness of the central mys-tery – we know the killer's identity from the teaser and the best the writers can do is withhold his motivation.

Apparently unhappy that his character shared so few scenes with Gillian Anderson, William B. Davis delivered the script for **En Ami**. In his last outing, Rob Bowman acquits himself well, ele-vating what could otherwise be a pulpy premise. After all these years, it is good to finally see Scully and the Cigarette Smoking Man on-screen together. Davis' script *almost* manages to convince us that his character has become genuinely benevolent. In the end though, after engineering a complex scheme to win Scully's trust, we are treated to yet another ambiguous conclusion, where the series' primary antagonist simply tosses the macguffin away. It's very well made, but at this stage of the series it would be more refreshing if CSM actually had changed his ways.

David Amann's script for **Chimera** doesn't pretend to be anything other than a creepy 'monster of the week' story, and the entire episode benefits from this lack of pretension. The idea of a mother so perfectly preened that her repressed emotions emerge as a murderous demon sounds like something that could have come from David Lynch. The central mystery intrigues, and even Scully's B-story has its moments. All up, a very watchable entry.

Gillian Anderson tries to offer up something new and fresh with **all things**. Unfortunately, the central story resembles a bunch of overly stylised, new age nonsense. One might be able to overlook this, but Scully's character in this episode is presented in a dramatically different way from the rest of the series – taking advice from spiritual healers, visiting Buddhist temples and having affairs with professors (not to mention scurrying out of Mulder's apartment half-dressed...) It's a frustrating and mystifying episode to watch, particularly as the series only chooses to shed light on these events retrospectively.

Brand X boasts a good performance from Tobin Bell, projecting quiet menace in spite of his character's meagre dialogue. The way Scully saves Mulder's life is a clever twist and there are some grisly corpses, but each death is so similar that after a while they lose all impact (especially the bugs coming out of the lawyer's mouth, proving again that season seven's CGI is well below the series' best). Overall, it feels like a by-the-numbers story relying too heavily on the shock value of its imagery.

After his successful directorial debut last season, there were high hopes for David Duchovny's **Hollywood A.D.** While the premise of a film based on the agents' investigations is interesting (and there are some good digs at the movie-making industry) the concept feels like it's being stretched to its limits. Given Mulder's usual disdain for religion, the central mystery (and the fact that Mulder entertains the idea of the 'Lazarus bowl' at all) seems very out of place. Everyone certainly appears to be having a good time, but that's rarely enough to maintain an audience's interest on its own. The series also reaches its visual effects nadir during the dancing skeleton sequence.

The low-point of the seventh season, **Fight Club** represents yet another attempt at quirkiness since the series' relocation to Los Angeles. Unfortunately, this entry is not only unfunny, but its central doppelganger narrative proves frustrating in the extreme. Opening with the lead actors' stand-ins might be passable as 'meta-humour' if the series hadn't already featured them in prominent guest roles (Anderson's stand-in plays Skinner's assistant, while Duchovny's stand-in appears as himself in 'Hungry').

The rest of the supporting cast is also incredibly grating. The quality of the series' other attempts at slapstick humour may be debatable, but 'Fight Club' is unquestionably a failure.

The concept of a genie lying dormant in an ancient rug demonstrates that **Je Souhaite** has its tongue planted firmly in cheek. By now, *The X-Files* has ceased to offer any pretence of a possible scientific explanation and instead it's simply updating old folklore. Vince Gilligan bravely tackles some big set-pieces in his directorial debut; the deserted city scenes are particularly impressive. The script is less successful, losing a bit of steam after Mulder is granted his three wishes. The whole story is pretty inconsequential, but it's handled well enough and makes for an amusing entry.

Capping off a disappointing season, **Requiem** marks a welcome return to the mythology and manages to inject some urgency into a series that by this point has become far too self-reflexive. Returning to the scene of the pilot, this entry doesn't exactly feel 'fresh' but it's still a welcome change of pace. The presence of so many returning characters brings an air of finality, but some of the supporting performances are very uneven. Despite the fact that the series would continue for a further two seasons, there is no doubt that *The X-Files* would be forever changed after this entry. While the ramifications of Scully's pregnancy won't become clear for some time, Mulder's abduction by aliens feels somehow appropriate. It's a strong cliffhanger, posing some exciting questions for the next season.

By season seven, it's fair to say that *The X-Files* was no longer "cool." The show certainly remained popular (even if ratings dipped this year), but after seven years on the air the series had firmly entered the mainstream and no longer captured the public's attention like it had a few years earlier. Some argue simplistically that *The X-Files* began to decline "as soon as Mulder left," but the truth is that David Duchovny's last full season is also one of the series' most disappointing. Far too many entries are wasted on self-indulgent and insubstantial material. Other than the premiere and the finale, season seven essentially vacates the series' long-standing mythology storyline. Samantha's disappearance may apparently have been resolved, but the tone of these episodes differs so dramatically from the rest of the mythology that the explanation proves unsatisfying.

Although there are many examples of *The X-Files* treading water this season, a glaring indicator of the series' creative lethargy is the fact that nearly *half* of these episodes are set within California. It's a symptom of narrative exhaustion when the series can no longer even pretend that its stories take place beyond the studio back-lot.

Off-screen, this year saw some notable departures. Rob Bowman, a director who had been with the show since the first season and contributed so much to the series' visual style, left mid-season. Experienced producer Michael Watkins also finished up with the series, having joined the production staff following the move to Los Angeles. One director who helmed several episodes this year was Thomas J. Wright (a veteran of Chris Carter's *Millennium*), who also departed before season's end. Writer Steven Maeda came onboard and would remain with the series until its conclusion. Michelle MacLaren (who would later collaborate with Vince Gilligan on *Breaking Bad*) also joined as a co-executive producer.

SEASON EIGHT

As the 'meat in the sandwich' of *The X-Files'* final three-part episode, **Within** faces similar challenges to other middle instalments.
The overwhelming focus on FBI office politics could very easily
have been dull, but this story benefits from introducing a major
new character. Robert Patrick's performance as John Doggett is a
bit too self-assured here, with few of the character's vulnerabilities
evident at this early stage. That's certainly no fault of the actor,
who manages to establish a lot on the basis of limited material.
This entry works best when it's dealing with these new story
threads. It's a shame then that so much time is devoted to reintroducing old characters that no one seemed to miss like Kersh and
Gibson Praise, and retrospectively diagnosing Mulder with a neurological illness is an ill-advised move by the writers. **Without**
thankfully dispenses with much of that material and instead turns
its attention to the search for Mulder. It's effectively paced and
well plotted, but where this episode excels is in its efforts to bring
Scully and Doggett's characters together. Not all fans embraced
this new direction, but these two episodes manage to imbue the
series with a renewed sense of urgency and provide as effective an
introduction for a new lead character as one could want.

Patience continues this year's back to basics approach, with Chris Carter delivering a very straightforward monster story. The only problem - it's a little too straightforward... The focus on scares is a welcome change from the lighter tone of the last two seasons, but it offers few real surprises. The make-up job on the man-bat antagonist isn't the series' best, and the sexism of the local cops seems like a tired retread of material we have seen before. While they can't match Anderson and Duchovny's chemistry, the scenes between Scully and Doggett are by far this entry's biggest asset.

Rather than introducing the series' new character, **Roadrunners** splits up the two leads and puts the focus squarely on Scully. *The X-Files* has always done small towns with something to hide very well, and the slug creature is a creepy antagonist. It is *very* gory for a Vince Gilligan episode, but the effects are impressive. When Doggett saves the day in the finale (clearly what the episode has been building to), it's a great device to bring him and Scully closer together. Unfortunately though, it's undercut in the very next scene – Doggett's dialogue coming across as a bit too condescending and insensitive.

It's been a while since the series served up a 'creepy kid' story, but **Invocation** reverses this trend. It's a strong mystery about a boy abducted years earlier who returns without having aged a day. The best moments are those dealing with the human drama of this premise – how should Billy's father and (younger) brother feel about his return? Unfortunately, these moments are few and far between, and the story stumbles when dealing the more paranormal aspects (the psychic who suffers a seizure feels particularly unnecessary). The opening flashback is beautifully shot and the story is a subtle way of introducing Doggett's own past trauma.

Redrum is as close to anthology storytelling as *The X-Files* will ever get. With the central characters largely absent, this entry focuses on a lawyer living each day in reverse. Take nothing away from Joe Morton (in a great performance), but it's a shame that this episode feels as if it could be transplanted into almost any other television show. Like 'Hungry,' when Scully and Doggett do turn up here they seem starkly out of place. Given all the recent efforts to establish John Doggett, this entry's heavy focus on a one-shot character feels like a missed opportunity.

Proof that *The X-Files* can still deliver a standout entry after so many years, **Via Negativa** has a wonderfully unsettling and creepy atmosphere. It's telling that scores of people die in the first few minutes here – while 'The Field Where I Died' looked at whether or not the agents could save the cult members in time, Frank Spotnitz's script is far more concerned with Doggett's inner struggle. With Gillian Anderson's screen time drastically reduced, Robert Patrick delivers an excellent performance of a man being slowly pushed to the brink. The central story about astral planes and third eyes may be a bit flimsy, but that hardly matters when the dream-like imagery is such a triumph. Brilliantly foreboding, this is one of the first genuinely scary entries in a long time.

Surekill and **Salvage** are ostensibly pretty similar stories, dealing with everyday blue-collar men who gain extraordinary abilities. In the former, an exterminator with x-ray vision fleeces local drug-dealers with the help of his odious twin brother. There are some cool visuals, like the sun filtering into a room riddled with bullet holes, but it offers precious little else. The premise is so paper-thin and the characters all so unsympathetic (especially Tammy, who the audience is apparently supposed to care about) that it's a tough episode to sit through. 'Salvage,' on the other hand, takes an equally pulpy premise and manages to fashion it into a solidly entertaining entry. The concept of a metal-man was apparently well advanced before Robert Patrick was cast, but the wink at the actor's most famous role is amusing. There are some other darkly comic moments (Ray eating aluminium foil and trimming his whiskers with nail clippers), but the story doesn't quite achieve the emotional heights it's aiming for. The plot may only be middling, but the direction, the make-up, and the effects all combine to offer up some arresting visuals.

Trying to tackle some pretty deep themes, **Badlaa** ends up being one of the eighth season's misfires. A legless Indian beggar crawling inside an obese American man in the teaser is enough to pique anyone's interest, but before long plot holes overwhelm John Shiban's script. If this character can take any form he chooses, why does he even need such a vessel in the first place? Viewers are repeatedly asked to accept that this guy can do pretty much anything the story requires him to because of... foreign mysticism, or something. The playful dialogue in the early scenes is also very at odds with the rest of the content, especially the overdramatic climax where Scully must effectively shoot a child.

In **The Gift**, Doggett investigates a 'soul eater' with a connection to Mulder. Despite the retrospective plot thread of Mulder's neurological illness being very problematic, 'The Gift' deals with it in perhaps the best possible way. In Scully's absence, the focus switches to Doggett and we actually learn more about his character than we do Mulder's. Particularly poignant is the final scene where the shadow of Mulder silently lingers over Doggett in the x-files office – it's an explicit acknowledgement of the character's struggle to fill Mulder's shoes, just as Patrick is doing an admirable job of distinguishing himself from Duchovny's portrayal.

Medusa doesn't pretend to be anything other than a straight-up action thriller. We've seen *The X-Files* do flesh-eating viruses before, but the tense set-up is this entry's biggest strength. A possible pathogen in the Boston subway inevitably leads to a climax where Doggett must jump out of the path of an oncoming train. Frank Spotnitz's script has just enough elements to keep the audience guessing about the nature of the mystery, while the scale of the production (on a television budget, no less) is impressive.

As with other episodes this year, **Per Manum** retcons the events of previous seasons. But unlike Mulder's mysterious illness, the flashbacks here to Scully's attempts at fertility treatment (with Mulder's help) are entirely necessary. It is good to see Scully's mysterious pregnancy *finally* being dealt with, although the writers effectively leave their options open with the final scene. The central 'alien babies' premise is flimsy, but 'Per Manum' deserves praise for organically bringing together long forgotten threads of the mythology stretching back to the fourth season, while introducing new characters like Knowle Rohrer. It's been a long time since the tone of the mythology episodes felt as consistent as this.

Mulder returns in a very unexpected manner in **This Is Not Happening** and **Deadalive**. The story picks up where the events of this season's premiere episodes left off. Abductees are being returned close to death, before being miraculously revived by Jeremiah Smith (last seen in 'Herrenvolk'). Monica Reyes' introduction in the first entry feels very tacked on; otherwise though this episode features some great sequences. Mark Snow's themes have rarely been better, and the stirring climax is even enough to make you overlook Scully's melodramatic final scream. 'Deadalive' opens with Mulder's funeral, and while the story is markedly different from its predecessor, the shift in tone feels natural. Like 'One Breath,' a story where one of the lead characters is unconscious in a hospital bed really shouldn't be this successful. The practical effects are top-notch, as are the performances (Doggett's confrontation with Krycek is a particular highlight). The ending – where Mulder is saved and cured of the alien virus by run-of-the-mill anti-virals – seems like a cop-out, but it's hard to criticise when the rest of the episode is as entertaining as this. Whereas 'Amor Fati' bludgeoned the audience with a heavy-handed "Mulder is Jesus Christ!" motif, this excellent two-parter succeeds by examining similar themes in a way that feels much more tonally consistent with the rest of the series.

Three Words essentially wraps-up a mythology arc that began with 'Per Manum.' Despite the plot's familiarity (particularly the sequence of Mulder infiltrating the social security administration with the help of the Lone Gunmen) it introduces enough new elements and is so briskly paced that you barely notice.

The strongest parts of this episode are not the mythology's ongoing contortions, but the depiction of Mulder's struggle to reenter his old life. It's handled very well, with Mulder's impetuous behaviour here subverting audience expectations of a heroic return. The performances are mostly excellent, but it's a shame that Duchovny can barely disguise his boredom with the role after he is *finally* given something substantial to do this season.

Empedocles works best when it is revealing further details about the abduction of Doggett's son. That being said, abruptly killing off the anonymous child molester responsible in the opening teaser seems misguided, and the series would wisely choose to revisit this storyline in greater depth next season. The central story – positing that evil is able to 'jump' from one person to the next in moments of weakness – allows for some great visuals, but it's also very silly. When the woman's eyes suddenly start glowing in the climax and she instantly turns homicidal, the ridiculousness of this concept is laid bare. While the interactions between Mulder, Doggett and Reyes are all compelling, it's a shame that the Mulder and Scully scenes that bookend this episode feel *very* forced.

Vienen is an outrageously high-concept episode about the crew of an oil rig who are surreptitiously harvesting black oil. Essentially ignoring many of the developments in the mythology over the last few years, this entry instead revisits the radioactive black oil from the third season. While the lapse in continuity could possibly cause some confusion, this story is so well paced and action-packed that any such nitpicking seems unfair. The effects are fantastic (aside from some average green screen shots in the climax) and it's impossible not to be impressed by the direction and production values on display here. Mulder and Doggett's verbal sparring is great, and by the end you truly believe that these two characters have developed a healthy respect for one another.

For his directorial debut, Frank Spotnitz's script for **Alone** keeps the central mystery very straightforward. The plot, about a half human/half salamander, is really just an excuse for a nostalgic stroll down memory lane. The character of Agent Harrison may appear to be the embodiment of every *X-Files* fan, but at times here she comes across as a little too cutesy and frustrating. The winking in-jokes are amusing, but the dark and creepy atmosphere is even more impressive. The story may not have any real twists or turns, but it's a perfectly entertaining entry for Duchovny's last standalone episode.

As was the case in season seven, it was unclear during production whether **Essence** and **Existence** would be the series' final instalments. Chris Carter obviously wasn't too concerned about wrapping up the series' many lingering story threads, instead fashioning an exciting two-parter that effectively serves as one long chase sequence. At first, 'Essence' meanders a little bit as everyone prepares for the birth of Scully's baby. These are the weakest scenes in the episode, as they feel achingly familiar following on the heels of 'Per Manum.' When Krycek shows up though, events really kick into high gear as Billy Miles (now an alien super-soldier) ruthlessly pursues Scully. It's an exciting climax, and the subtle cliffhanger is effective. 'Existence' promptly restages the same chase sequence within the FBI, all while the super-soldiers close in on Scully. In some ways, both these episodes are very alike but the events are so exhilirating, and the pace so relentless, that it hardly seems to matter. The super-soldier arc will never again be as strong as it is here, but the similarities between these two entries should serve as a warning that this plotline offers very little substance beyond some superficial action scenes. All in all, this two-parter does a great job of concluding the season.

Season eight represents a welcome return to form for *The X-Files*. While the introduction of John Doggett understandably had some fans wary, the producers thankfully chose to refocus on the dark atmosphere and scary stories that the series was famous for. While there may still be some plodding standalone instalments, on the whole, the back to basics approach works. The search for Mulder also reinvigorated the series' mythology, bringing an urgency to these episodes that had been missing for several seasons. The second-half of season eight is notable for almost completely serializing the show, with nearly every episode adding new recurring characters and requiring detailed knowledge of the previous week's events. It's a bold move, but these episodes are so tonally consistent that they make for rewarding viewing.

Apart from the writers, credit should go to Robert Patrick for establishing his character so quickly and effectively. Perhaps unsurprisingly, David Duchovny seemed a bit bored this season, although Gillian Anderson continued to deliver strong performances that connect these episodes with those that have come before. The eighth season was a time of flux for *The X-Files*, but it's difficult to think of a better way than this for the series to make its transition.

Aside from the departure of Jeffrey Bell, the writing staff remained fairly stable this year. Kim Manners continued to act as a directorial stalwart, single-handedly directing a third of this year's episodes. He was joined in the director's chair by Tony Wharmby, who would also return for the final season. While guest directors Rod Hardy and Richard Compton helmed some strong episodes, neither would make any further contribution to the series after season eight.

SEASON NINE

With no real cliffhanger from last year, the final season of *The X-Files* kicks off with the two-parter of **Nothing Important Happened Today** and **Nothing Important Happened Today II**. The title is unfortunate, given how difficult it is to pinpoint any significant moments that occur during either episode. We do get the introduction of Cary Elwes as Brad Follmer, but his character is so frustratingly underwritten that he adds very little. The plot is further weakened by focusing on Kersh, a character who has always been depicted as an ambitious bureaucrat, with none of Skinner's innate decency and moral conflict. Then there is the fleeting appearance of "Mulder" in Scully's shower... an incongruous shot that only serves to remind viewers that David Duchovny is now gone for good. At this stage, it's become impossible for viewers to divorce the on-screen narrative from the series' production. The best the writers can do is to address these production issues in a way that feels consistent with what has come before – Mulder's abduction in season eight proved a successful example of this, but his completely unexplained (and apparently voluntary) disappearance here is a bridge too far. Unwilling to kill off or recast the character, the producers' decision to retcon an explanation for

Mulder's disappearance stretches credibility far more than the central narrative about tainted water and super-soldiers. Aside from the dodgy CGI shot of the ship in the second episode's teaser, the production itself is well handled with some impressive set-pieces. Unfortunately, the stakes here are so low that it's difficult to get invested in the plot at all.

Frank Spotnitz returns to the director's chair in **Dæmonicus**, an intriguing episode that thankfully dispenses with the mythology to focus on a case of demonic possession. This instalment offers a more cerebral story than 'Alone,' allowing Spotnitz to indulge in a few stylish directing choices. While some of these flourishes are more successful than others, the chessboard motif is particularly impressive. The plot is sluggishly paced, but it succeeds on the back of a strong performance from James Remar and a wonderfully tense atmosphere. The contrast between the many understated, dialogue-free sequences and the outrageously over-the-top scene of Kobold projectile-vomiting on Doggett is brilliant. An underrated gem.

4-D deals with the concept of alternative dimensions, and in doing so it manages to explore a lot more of Doggett and Reyes' characters than other episodes this season will allow. The interactions between Robert Patrick and Annabeth Gish are the highlights, suggesting that they could share some genuine chemistry if only they had the right script. The premise is intriguing at first, and the dimension-hopping images are cool, but the ending wraps things up far too conveniently. Seeing a serial killer feed his mother human tongues is also extremely unsettling, even for *The X-Files*.

The show serves up its final 'angsty teen' story with **Lord of the Flies**, and it's a good example of how much the passage of time has impacted *The X-Files*. While the series never exactly portrayed its teenage characters faithfully, in years past they were at least more interesting than they are here. The teenagers on this show now resemble models and their crushes are downright Shakespearean. Aaron Paul at least gives an early hint of his charisma, even if his character is written as a frustrating brat. The reality television concept intrigues for a moment, but there's nowhere for this idea to go following the teaser. The competing elements of quirky humour, body horror and teen love story quickly sink this disappointing outing.

If 'Nothing Important Happened Today' made the mistake of providing no credible explanation for Mulder's disappearance, **Trust No 1** compounds this error by devoting an entire episode to this storyline and offering very little new information. The characterisation is all over the place here – Mulder and Scully's emails sound nothing like the characters we have come to know. We're also blithely informed that they slept together *two seasons ago* in 'all things.' However, the fundamental flaw with this episode is its attempt to dramatise the prospect of Mulder's return. The premise is doomed to failure given that both the producers and the audience know it's just a tease. When "Mulder" does appear, the extreme long shot of a stand-in running away from Scully would be laughable if it didn't feel like such a betrayal of his character. The biggest shame is that this episode's theme of increasingly pervasive electronic surveillance was so ahead of its time. This storyline might have actually proved interesting, but it's never examined in any detail.

Much like 'X-Cops,' **John Doe** is a stylishly produced entry with a fairly ordinary mystery, but Vince Gilligan deserves great credit for the inventive central premise. The idea of Doggett waking up in a Mexican town with no memory of who he is or how he got there is inspired, and Robert Patrick delivers a truly great performance. The ultimate explanation of a 'memory vampire' may be a little underwhelming, but the emotional call-back to the disappearance of Doggett's son means it's easily overlooked. Plaudits should go to Michelle MacLaren for the gritty, overexposed look of the episode, which contributes immeasurably to the atmosphere and foreshadows some of the stylistic choices that would go on to be used so successfully in Gilligan's *Breaking Bad*.

Hellbound proves to be an unexpectedly entertaining entry about reincarnated souls that's notable for finally exploring Reyes' character in greater depth. Although it shares narrative similarities to 'The Field Where I Died,' the lengthy monologues of that entry are jettisoned here in favour of a wonderfully creepy atmosphere. Instead of attempting to do too much, this entry wisely depicts the characters' past lives in very broad strokes. Admittedly the scenes of victims being skinned alive are very gory, but the effect is achieved very well and Kim Manners' direction is superb.

The mythology episodes of *The X-Files* were once the show's most eagerly anticipated instalments, but **Provenance** and **Providence** demonstrate how confused and impenetrable these stories have become. The plot throws up many elements that we've seen the series do better elsewhere – UFO cults, buried spacecraft and alien rubbings – in the hope that something will stick. There's some confused dialogue about ancient prophecies, as this season once again takes the ill-advised route of making Mulder central to proceedings in which his character can play no part. The rest of the story's focus on William is equally unfortunate, as we're asked to sympathise with a character lacking any possible motivation. Doggett and Reyes simply react to events in these episodes, while Scully is written as such a shrill, panicky mother that it feels like a waste of Gillian Anderson's considerable talents. The mythology has always been dense, but in the past you could at least rely on these episodes to provide some impressive set-pieces. For the most part though, even the action sequences here are dull. The exception is the second instalment's glorious teaser – this fleetingly brilliant Gulf War flashback demonstrates that the series could still say something interesting about the real world if it had the courage to tackle such material. As impressive as that one sequence is, it can't save this dull and dreary two-parter.

Audrey Pauley shows that, despite some slip ups, the series' central concept remains fundamentally strong. Tracey Ellis from 'Oubliette' returns to play the titular character, the only person able to communicate with the souls of hospital patients trapped in a ghostly netherworld. Reyes' car crash in the opening scene is a shock, as are the revelations of the murderous doctor's crimes. The dream-like imagery of purgatory is pitch-perfect, and Annabeth Gish relishes the overdue focus on her character. Full credit though must go to Robert Patrick, who portrays Doggett here with just the right hint of vulnerability.

John Shiban's first (and only) directing credit, **Underneath** reportedly had the network worried during production. It's a testament to all involved that the finished product betrays none of these issues. The episode itself is fairly unremarkable; it's a solid story about a killer from Doggett's past who is exonerated by DNA evidence years later. The twist is very obvious, but Shiban at least manages to generate a creepy atmosphere. Some moments (like the killer appearing in the mirror) feel very familiar, but they're effective nonetheless. The production crew do a fine job constructing the elaborate sewer set, and it is good to get a brief glimpse of Doggett in his NYPD days.

Chris Carter's last directorial outing before the second movie, **Improbable** is a bizarre yet amusing entry about numerology. Featuring the music of Karl Zéro and an appearance from Burt Reynolds, it's safe to say that this is unlike many other x-files. The central theme of hidden meanings that we could all see if only we knew where to look may be intriguing, but it doesn't feel like it's enough to sustain an entire episode. Instead, we're treated to scenes of Scully and Reyes playing checkers, carnivals, Burt Reynolds dancing, along with two old men lip-syncing. It's all very whimsical, but when people are being murdered this sort of tone lowers the stakes considerably, and it feels very out of place in an otherwise gloomily sombre season.

Scary Monsters is a solid little entry, focusing on a child whose imagination is so vivid that he can bring his nightmares to life. The snowbound scenes in Pennsylvania have a wonderful atmosphere, but it's nicely offset by the lighter scenes in Scully's apartment. The escalating weirdness of the young boy's visions provides some very effective scares, so it's a bit of a shame that the computer generated monsters of the title are not at all convincing. Still, it's a nice spin on the isolation stories that the series has always done so effectively.

As with season seven's 'Millennium,' **Jump the Shark** feels like an episode of another show masquerading as an x-file. The failure of the Lone Gunmen's self-titled spin-off series is proof that while there may be some humour to be derived from *The X-Files* universe, it is most definitely *not* a comedy series. This instalment suffers from the same goofy tone of *The Lone Gunmen* series, while trying to balance it alongside a deadly serious plot, and shoehorning in the cast of *The X-Files* for good measure. The end result feels very out of place within not only this season, but the series proper. That being said, the trio's final sacrifice is one of the few highlights of the episode, wisely dispensing with the slapstick.

The storyline of Scully's baby thankfully concludes with **William**. Although this saga has continued now for almost two seasons, its fundamental weaknesses have only become glaringly obvious this year – an infant will never be a compelling central character as he's impossible for the audience to relate to. As a nursing mother, Scully's character has also been reduced to a screaming wreck too often this season (most notably in 'Provenance' and 'Providence'). Appropriately then, this episode opts to move on. The central storyline of a disfigured "Mulder" returning is yet another example of the series foregrounding an absent character, and it's not a particularly convincing bluff. David Duchovny's direction proves much more anonymous in this outing than previous efforts, but his brief cameo is a welcome surprise. While Gillian Anderson delivers a great performance, the rest of the episode is quite understated (at least until the sappy conclusion).

With the series now tying up loose ends, **Release** thankfully tackles the story of Doggett's murdered son and, in doing so, finally realises the potential of this arc. It's a gorgeously shot episode and well acted, with Mark Snow's excellent score making it a joy to watch. Cary Elwes as Follmer is finally given something to do here, and then promptly written out of the series. The interstitial titles might have felt pretentious in any other episode, but they work well here. The scene of the SWAT team arresting Hayes brilliantly encapsulates everything successful about this entry in a single scene. It's interesting to consider whether this season might have flourished if only the series had embraced the more lyrical style of this entry, instead of opting to continue the series' well-worn formula with new cast members.

Some criticise the series' second-to-last episode, **Sunshine Days**, for focusing incongruously on *The Brady Bunch* while neglecting *The X-Files'* many unanswered questions. It's true that Vince Gilligan's central story falls a bit flat. The production crew may do a superb job of realizing the Brady house, but the pacing is deathly slow before it's all wrapped up very quickly. It certainly has its flaws, but 'Sunshine Days' works best as an ambitious allegory of the fans' passion for this series, and a paean to the medium of television itself. The antagonist, Oliver, refuses to let go of his favourite show to the extent that he is more comfortable inhabiting this fantasy world than moving on with his life. The reference to an unpopular character introduced late in the series' broadcast just to boost flagging ratings is also particularly topical. It's not perfect, but when viewed in context it seems like an appropriate entry to cap off the series.

After nine seasons and more than two hundred episodes, *The X-Files* television series concludes with **The Truth**. The final entry begins promisingly with an exciting action scene, and the sequence depicting Mulder's detention presciently foreshadows the real-life injustices of Guantanamo Bay. Disappointingly though, the proceedings grind to a halt when Mulder's trial begins. These scenes, where the history of the mythology is laid out in painstaking detail, actually do a good job of bringing together the many disparate threads of this arc, but they're interminably dull.

Mulder's cringe-inducing courtroom speech about "the truth" doesn't assist matters at all. It's also galling that Scully is given so little to do here, while Doggett and Reyes are especially under-served. After a season spent focusing on an absent character, this entry is too quick to ignore those characters who have been present for more recent events. The climactic action sequence and the reappearance of the Cigarette Smoking Man reenergise proceedings a little, but these scenes are only tenuously connected to the preceding events. As you would expect, the production is flawless and Kim Manners toils admirably to invest the courtroom scenes with some drama. It's nostalgic to see some old favourites return – X and Krycek's cameos are particular highlights – but it's best not to think about their relationship to the plot for too long (Krycek's heroic act is to hold a door open? And how does X hand Mulder a piece of paper!?) Ultimately, while some elements may work, the whole plot device of Mulder's trial proves misguided. Likewise, the religiosity of Mulder and Scully's final conversation seems strangely out of place. As the series' final word on the mysteries that have intrigued us for nine years, one can't help but be disap-pointed at the manner in which 'The Truth' wraps things up.

The final season does not have a great reputation among viewers. While this year definitely contains some weak entries, in reality it also features a few hidden gems. In the wake of 9/11, the series seems to have made a conscious decision to adopt more of an an-thology format, with fewer straightforward x-file investigations, and more entries where the central characters actually experience paranormal events themselves (think, '4-D,' 'John Doe,' 'Audrey Pauley'). Season nine is at its best when presenting new material with the same moody atmosphere and dark style for which *The X-Files* is famous. Conversely, there's no doubt that it's at its worst when focusing an inordinate amount of attention on plotlines and characters from years gone by. The series is no longer the same show it was then and, rather than allowing *The X-Files* to reinvent itself, these stories simply draw the viewer's attention to how much things have changed.

As the only remaining performers from the series' early days, Gillian Anderson and Mitch Pileggi do the best they can with the material they're given. While Pileggi is finally given lead status this year, Anderson's contribution in some of these episodes is reduced to a single scene. Robert Patrick continued to impress as Doggett and, to his credit, that character feels far more familiar than he should in only his second season. Annabeth Gish has some strong outings as Reyes, but the writers too often burden her with weak material. The characterisation of Reyes has never been entirely consistent – first introduced as an expert on the occult, she later became a ditzy new-age hippy, before morphing this year into a more gullible version of Mulder. It's telling however that those episodes which shed more light on Doggett and Reyes were some of this season's strongest.

Season nine features a number of guest directors, with Kim Manners contributing the lion's share of the episodes. Aside from the various writers who moonlighted as directors this year, Tony Wharmby and Cliff Bole were the only two directors who had previously contributed episodes to the series. As for the writing staff, Thomas Schnauz contributed two scripts this year, and he would go on to collaborate with Vince Gilligan on *Breaking Bad* along with several other members of the production crew.

Two crew members who made significant contributions to the show over the entirety of its nine year run are Paul Rabwin and Mark Snow. Primarily responsible for overseeing post-production, Rabwin's influence is most visible in the series' cinematic special effects and editing. While Snow is most associated with the series' signature theme tune, his episodic scores also formed a large part of the series' success. Much of his early music consisted of atmospheric sound design, but in later seasons his scores began to incorporate some beautifully melodic material.

I WANT TO BELIEVE

Coming ten years after the first movie, **I Want To Believe** attempts to please those who argued that *The X-Files'* dense mythology was never as strong as the standalone stories. The trouble with this argument is that the episodic nature of the television show compensated for the occasional lapse in quality – for every superb standalone mystery, there were several others that were merely adequate, and a few that were awful. That's perfectly fine when the audience is being treated to a new episode each week, but as a one-off event, a feature film is necessarily judged more harshly. Had it been just one entry in a season of twenty or more episodes, 'I Want To Believe' may have escaped some of the harsh criticism it received upon its release. As the first entry in the canon for six years though, it is a disappointment.

Chris Carter's direction can't compete with the epic visual style of Rob Bowman, but he does sporadically make use of the broader cinematic canvas. The use of intercutting in the opening is effective, serving to make the sequence more exciting than it perhaps should have been. By returning to Canada, the movie is also able to make use of some ominous, snowy vistas. Otherwise though, 'I Want To Believe' lacks the first movie's ambitious sense of scale and grandeur, with even Mark Snow's score feeling somewhat muted. Of course, this is partly a function of this movie's significantly reduced budget. Nevertheless, given how far the television series managed to stretch its limited resources, it's surprising that this outing isn't able to achieve better.

The acting is solid, with Gillian Anderson impressive as usual and David Duchovny finally managing to overcome the look of boredom that marred his last few years on the series. Billy Connolly may have been an unorthodox choice for Father Joe, but his performance is a highlight amongst an otherwise average supporting cast. Agents Whitney and Drummy are cookie-cutter characters that we've seen many times before, and the villains are severely underdeveloped. Having said that, Mitch Pilleggi's cameo as Skinner is a fun and welcome surprise, providing a sorely needed lift in the final act.

The writing team of Chris Carter & Frank Spotnitz was one of the television series' most dependable; consistently entertaining and intriguing, and occasionally achieving brilliance. It's a shame, therefore, that the script is probably this film's biggest weakness (no doubt exacerbated by the writers' strike that occurred during production). While the first movie necessarily had to excise some mythology plot elements for the sake of time and coherence, this story feels like it's labouring to include material just to pad out the running time to feature length. The most egregious example of this is the secondary plotline about Scully's struggle to treat a young boy. It's a superfluous thread, only tenuously connected to the main plot, and at times it rivals the main x-file for ridiculousness (Scully, a trained pathologist, consults an internet search engine before undertaking life-saving surgery?).

To the film's credit, the characters here feel fully realised – Mulder and Scully have aged just like the audience, and we find them in a very different place from the events of the series. But while this may be authentic, it's not particularly entertaining. Without denying the importance of the leads, Carter was right when he said that this series has always been about Mulder and Scully's dealings with the paranormal, and not solely about the characters' private lives. When the central mystery is as familiar and ordinary as this though, it becomes difficult to get too invested in the characters.

Perhaps the real shame about this movie is that it manages to recreate the visual style of *The X-Files* effectively enough, but the overall tone is far bleaker than the series ever was. The central message of the film – "don't give up" – seems much more world-weary and pessimistic than the youthful rebelliousness of the television series. In this way, the baffling post-credits shot of Mulder and Scully breaking the fourth wall to wave at the audience may be a sort of concession; evidence that even the filmmakers recognised that this story was a grimmer coda than these two characters deserved.

EPISODE LIST

Entries are listed in order of their original U.S. broadcast date.
Episode numbers refer to the order in which each episode was aired
(not the episode's individual production code).

Season One

	Title	Writer(s)	Director	Originally Broadcast
1X01	Pilot	Chris Carter	Robert Mandel	10 Sept 1993
1X02	Deep Throat	Chris Carter	Daniel Sackheim	17 Sept 1993
1X03	Squeeze	Glen Morgan & James Wong	Harry Longstreet	24 Sept 1993
1X04	Conduit	Alex Gansa & Howard Gordon	Daniel Sackheim	1 Oct 1993
1X05	The Jersey Devil	Chris Carter	Joe Napolitano	8 Oct 1993
1X06	Shadows	Glen Morgan & James Wong	Michael Katleman	22 Oct 1993
1X07	Ghost in the Machine	Alex Gansa & Howard Gordon	Jerrold Freedman	29 Oct 1993
1X08	Ice	Glen Morgan & James Wong	David Nutter	5 Nov 1993
1X09	Space	Chris Carter	William Graham	12 Nov 1993
1X10	Fallen Angel	Alex Gansa & Howard Gordon	Larry Shaw	19 Nov 1993
1X11	Eve	Kenneth Biller & Chris Brancato	Fred Gerber	10 Dec 1993
1X12	Fire	Chris Carter	Larry Shaw	17 Dec 1993
1X13	Beyond the Sea	Glen Morgan & James Wong	David Nutter	7 Jan 1994
1X14	Genderbender	Larry Barber & Paul Barber	Rob Bowman	21 Jan 1994
1X15	Lazarus	Alex Gansa & Howard Gordon	David Nutter	4 Feb 1994

1X16	Young at Heart	Scott Kaufer and Chris Carter	Michael Lange	11 Feb 1994
1X17	E.B.E.	Glen Morgan & James Wong	William Graham	18 Feb 1994
1X18	Miracle Man	Chris Carter & Howard Gordon	Michael Lange	18 Mar 1994
1X19	Shapes	Marilyn Osborn	David Nutter	1 Apr 1994
1X20	Darkness Falls	Chris Carter	Joe Napolitano	15 Apr 1994
1X21	Tooms	Glen Morgan & James Wong	David Nutter	22 Apr 1994
1X22	Born Again	Alex Gansa & Howard Gordon	Jerrold Freedman	29 Apr 1994
1X23	Roland	Chris Ruppenthal	David Nutter	6 May 1994
1X24	The Erlenmeyer Flask	Chris Carter	R.W. Goodwin	13 May 1994

Season Two

	Title	Writer(s)	Director	Originally Broadcast
2X01	Little Green Men	Glen Morgan & James Wong	David Nutter	16 Sept 1994
2X02	The Host	Chris Carter	Daniel Sackheim	23 Sept 1994
2X03	Blood	Glen Morgan & James Wong (Story by Darin Morgan)	David Nutter	30 Sept 1994
2X04	Sleepless	Howard Gordon	Rob Bowman	7 Oct 1994
2X05	Duane Barry	Chris Carter	Chris Carter	14 Oct 1994
2X06	Ascension	Paul Brown	Michael Lange	21 Oct 1994
2X07	3	Chris Ruppenthal and Glen Morgan & James Wong	David Nutter	4 Nov 1994
2X08	One Breath	Glen Morgan & James Wong	R.W. Goodwin	11 Nov 1994

2X09	Firewalker	Howard Gordon	David Nutter	18 Nov 1994
2X10	Red Museum	Chris Carter	Win Phelps	9 Dec 1994
2X11	Excelsius Dei	Paul Brown	Stephen Surjik	16 Dec 1994
2X12	Aubrey	Sarah B. Charno	Rob Bowman	6 Jan 1995
2X13	Irresistible	Chris Carter	David Nutter	13 Jan 1995
2X14	Die Hand Die Verletzt	Glen Morgan & James Wong	Kim Manners	27 Jan 1995
2X15	Fresh Bones	Howard Gordon	Rob Bowman	3 Feb 1995
2X16	Colony	Chris Carter (Story by David Duchovny & Chris Carter)	Nick Marck	10 Feb 1995
2X17	End Game	Frank Spotnitz	Rob Bowman	17 Feb 1995
2X18	Fearful Symmmetry	Steve De Jarnatt	James Whitmore Jr	24 Feb 1995
2X19	Død Kalm	Howard Gordon & Alex Gansa (Story by Howard Gordon)	Rob Bowman	10 Mar 1995
2X20	Humbug	Darin Morgan	Kim Manners	31 Mar 1995
2X21	The Calusari	Sarah B. Charno	Michael Vejar	14 Apr 1995
2X22	F. Emasculata	Chris Carter & Howard Gordon	Rob Bowman	28 Apr 1995
2X23	Soft Light	Vince Gilligan	James Contner	5 May 1995
2X24	Our Town	Frank Spotnitz	Rob Bowman	12 May 1995
2X25	Anasazi	Chris Carter (Story by David Duchovny & Chris Carter)	R.W. Goodwin	19 May 1995

Season Three

	Title	Writer(s)	Director	Originally Broadcast
3X01	The Blessing Way	Chris Carter	R.W. Goodwin	22 Sept 1995
3X02	Paper Clip	Chris Carter	Rob Bowman	29 Sept 1995
3X03	D.P.O.	Howard Gordon	Kim Manners	6 Oct 1995
3X04	Clyde Bruckman's Final Repose	Darin Morgan	David Nutter	13 Oct 1995
3X05	The List	Chris Carter	Chris Carter	20 Oct 1995
3X06	2Shy	Jeffrey Vlaming	David Nutter	3 Nov 1995
3X07	The Walk	John Shiban	Rob Bowman	10 Nov 1995
3X08	Oubliette	Charles Grant Craig	Kim Manners	17 Nov 1995
3X09	Nisei	Chris Carter, Howard Gordon & Frank Spotnitz	David Nutter	24 Nov 1995
3X10	731	Frank Spotnitz	Rob Bowman	1 Dec 1995
3X11	Revelations	Kim Newton	David Nutter	15 Dec 1995
3X12	War of the Coprophages	David Morgan	Kim Manners	5 Jan 1996
3X13	Syzgy	Chris Carter	Rob Bowman	26 Jan 1995
3X14	Grotesque	Howard Gordon	Kim Manners	2 Feb 1996
3X15	Piper Maru	Chris Carter & Frank Spotnitz	Rob Bowman	9 Feb 1996
3X16	Apocrypha	Chris Carter & Frank Spotnitz	Kim Manners	16 Feb 1996
3X17	Pusher	Vince Gilligan	Rob Bowman	23 Feb 1996

3X18	Teso Dos Bichos	John Shiban	Kim Manners	8 Mar 1996
3X19	Hell Money	Jeffrey Vlaming	Tucker Gates	29 Mar 1996
3X20	Jose Chung's *From Outer Space*	Darin Morgan	Rob Bowman	12 Apr 1996
3X21	Avatar	Howard Gordon (Story by David Duchovny & Howard Gordon)	James Charleston	26 Apr 1996
3X22	Quagmire	Kim Newton	Kim Manners	3 May 1996
3X23	Wetwired	Mat Beck	Rob Bowman	10 May 1996
3X24	Talitha Cumi	Chris Carter (Story by David Duchovny & Chris Carter)	R.W. Goodwin	17 May 1996

Season Four

	Title	Writer(s)	Director	Originally Broadcast
4X01	Herrenvolk	Chris Carter	R.W. Goodwin	4 Oct 1996
4X02	Home	Glen Morgan & James Wong	Kim Manners	11 Oct 1996
4X03	Teliko	Howard Gordon	James Charleston	18 Oct 1996
4X04	Unruhe	Vince Gilligan	Rob Bowman	27 Oct 1996
4X05	The Field Where I Died	Glen Morgan & James Wong	Rob Bowman	3 Nov 1996
4X06	Sanguinarium	Valerie Mayhew & Vivian Mayhew	Kim Manners	10 Nov 1996
4X07	Musings of a Cigarette Smoking Man	Glen Morgan	James Wong	17 Nov 1996
4X08	Tunguska	Chris Carter & Frank Spotnitz	Kim Manners	24 Nov 1996

4X09	Terma	Chris Carter & Frank Spotnitz	Rob Bowman	1 Dec 1996
4X10	Paper Hearts	Vince Gilligan	Rob Bowman	15 Dec 1996
4X11	El Mundo Gira	John Shiban	Tucker Gates	12 Jan 1997
4X12	Leonard Betts	Vince Gilligan, John Shiban & Frank Spotnitz	Kim Manners	26 Jan 1997
4X13	Never Again	Glen Morgan & James Wong	Rob Bowman	2 Feb 1997
4X14	Memento Mori	Chris Carter, Vince Gilligan, John Shiban & Frank Spotnitz	Rob Bowman	9 Feb 1997
4X15	Kaddish	Howard Gordon	Kim Manners	16 Feb 1997
4X16	Unrequited	Howard Gordon & Chris Carter (Story by Howard Gordon)	Michael Lange	23 Feb 1997
4X17	Tempus Fugit	Chris Carter & Frank Spotnitz	Rob Bowman	16 Mar 1997
4X18	Max	Chris Carter & Frank Spotnitz	Kim Manners	23 Mar 1997
4X19	Synchrony	Howard Gordon & David Greenwalt	James Charleston	13 Apr 1997
4X20	Small Potatoes	Vince Gilligan	Cliff Bole	20 Apr 1997
4X21	Zero Sum	Howard Gordon & Frank Spotnitz	Kim Manners	27 Apr 1997
4X22	Elegy	John Shiban	James Charleston	4 May 1997
4X23	Demons	R.W. Goodwin	Kim Manners	11 May 1997
4X24	Gethsemane	Chris Carter	R.W. Goodwin	18 May 1997

Season Five

	Title	Writer(s)	Director	Originally Broadcast
5X01	Redux	Chris Carter	R.W. Goodwin	2 Nov 1997
5X02	Redux II	Chris Carter	Kim Manners	9 Nov 1997
5X03	Unusual Suspects	Vince Gilligan	Kim Manners	16 Nov 1997
5X04	Detour	Frank Spotnitz	Brett Dowler	23 Nov 1997
5X05	The Post-Modern Prometheus	Chris Carter	Chris Carter	30 Nov 1997
5X06	Christmas Carol	Vince Gilligan, John Shiban & Frank Spotnitz	Peter Markle	7 Dec 1997
5X07	Emily	Vince Gilligan, John Shiban & Frank Spotnitz	Kim Manners	14 Dec 1997
5X08	Kitsunegari	Vince Gilligan & Tim Minear	Daniel Sackheim	4 Jan 1998
5X09	Schizogeny	Jessica Scott & Mike Wollaeger	Ralph Hemecker	11 Jan 1998
5X10	Chinga	Stephen King & Chris Carter	Kim Manners	8 Feb 1998
5X11	Kill Switch	William Gibson & Tom Maddox	Rob Bowman	15 Feb 1998
5X12	Bad Blood	Vince Gilligan	Cliff Bole	22 Feb 1998
5X13	Patient X	Chris Carter & Frank Spotnitz	Kim Manners	1 Mar 1998
5X14	The Red and The Black	Chris Carter & Frank Spotnitz	Chris Carter	8 Mar 1998
5X15	Travelers	John Shiban & Frank Spotnitz	William A. Graham	29 Mar 1998
5X16	Mind's Eye	Tim Minear	Kim Manners	19 Apr 1998

5X17	All Souls	John Shiban & Frank Spotnitz (Story by Billy Brown & Dan Angel)	Allen Coulter	26 Apr 1998
5X18	The Pine Bluff Variant	John Shiban	Rob Bowman	3 May 1998
5X19	Folie à Deux	Vince Gilligan	Kim Manners	10 May 1998
5X20	The End	Chris Carter	R.W. Goodwin	17 May 1998

Feature Film

Title	Writer(s)	Director	U.S. Release Date
The X-Files: Fight the Future	Chris Carter (Story by Chris Carter & Frank Spotnitz)	Rob Bowman	19 June 1998

Season Six

	Title	Writer(s)	Director	Originally Broadcast
6X01	The Beginning	Chris Carter	Kim Manners	8 Nov 1998
6X02	Drive	Vince Gilligan	Rob Bowman	15 Nov 1998
6X03	Triangle	Chris Carter	Chris Carter	22 Nov 1998
6X04	Dreamland	Vince Gilligan, John Shiban & Frank Spotnitz	Kim Manners	29 Nov 1998
6X05	Dreamland II	Vince Gilligan, John Shiban & Frank Spotnitz	Michael Watkins	6 Dec 1998
6X06	How the Ghosts Stole Christmas	Chris Carter	Chris Carter	13 Dec 1998
6X07	Terms of Endearment	David Amann	Rob Bowman	3 Jan 1999
6X08	Rain King	Jeffrey Bell	Kim Manners	10 Jan 1999
6X09	S.R. 819	John Shiban	Daniel Sackheim	17 Jan 1999

	Title	Writer(s)	Director	Originally Broadcast
6X10	Tithonus	Vince Gilligan	Michael Watkins	24 Jan 1999
6X11	Two Fathers	Chris Carter & Frank Spotnitz	Kim Manners	7 Feb 1999
6X12	One Son	Chris Carter & Frank Spotnitz	Rob Bowman	14 Feb 1999
6X13	Agua Mala	David Amann	Rob Bowman	21 Feb 1999
6X14	Monday	Vince Gilligan & John Shiban	Kim Manners	28 Feb 1999
6X15	Arcadia	Daniel Arkin	Michael Watkins	7 Mar 1999
6X16	Alpha	Jeffrey Bell	Peter Markle	28 Mar 1999
6X17	Trevor	Ken Hawryliw & Jim Guttridge	Rob Bowman	11 Apr 1999
6X18	Milagro	Chris Carter (Story by John Shiban & Frank Spotnitz)	Kim Manners	18 Apr 1999
6X19	The Unnatural	David Duchovny	David Duchovny	25 Apr 1999
6X20	Three of a Kind	Vince Gilligan & John Shiban	Bryan Spicer	2 May 1999
6X21	Field Trip	John Shiban & Vince Gilligan (Story by Frank Spotnitz)	Kim Manners	9 May 1999
6X22	Biogenesis	Chris Carter & Frank Spotnitz	Rob Bowman	16 May 1999

Season Seven

	Title	Writer(s)	Director	Originally Broadcast
7X01	The Sixth Extinction	Chris Carter	Kim Manners	7 Nov 1999
7X02	The Sixth Extinction II: Amor Fati	Chris Carter & David Duchovny	Michael Watkins	14 Nov 1999
7X03	Hungry	Vince Gilligan	Kim Manners	21 Nov 1999

7X04	Millennium	Vince Gilligan & John Shiban	Thomas J. Wright	28 Nov 1999
7X05	Rush	David Amann	Robert Lieberman	5 Dec 1999
7X06	The Goldberg Variation	Jeffrey Bell	Thomas J. Wright	12 Dec 1999
7X07	Orison	Chip Johannessen	Rob Bowman	9 Jan 2000
7X08	The Amazing Maleeni	Vince Gilligan, John Shiban & Frank Spotnitz	Thomas J. Wright	16 Jan 2000
7X09	Signs and Wonders	Jeffrey Bell	Kim Manners	23 Jan 2000
7X10	Sein Und Zeit	Chris Carter & Frank Spotnitz	Michael Watkins	6 Feb 2000
7X11	Closure	Chris Carter & Frank Spotnitz	Kim Manners	13 Feb 2000
7X12	X-Cops	Vince Gilligan	Michael Watkins	20 Feb 2000
7X13	First Person Shooter	William Gibson & Tom Maddox	Chris Carter	27 Feb 2000
7X14	Theef	Vince Gilligan, John Shiban & Frank Spotnitz	Kim Manners	12 Mar 2000
7X15	En Ami	William B. Davis	Rob Bowman	19 Mar 2000
7X16	Chimera	David Amann	Cliff Bole	2 Apr 2000
7X17	all things	Gillian Anderson	Gillian Anderson	9 Apr 2000
7X18	Brand X	Steven Maeda & Greg Walker	Kim Manners	16 Apr 2000
7X19	Hollywood A.D.	David Duchovny	David Duchovny	30 Apr 2000
7X20	Fight Club	Chris Carter	Paul Shapiro	7 May 2000
7X21	Je Souhaite	Vince Gilligan	Vince Gilligan	14 May 2000
7X22	Requiem	Chris Carter	Kim Manners	21 May 2000

Season Eight

	Title	Writer(s)	Director	Originally Broadcast
8X01	Within	Chris Carter	Kim Manners	5 Nov 2000
8X02	Without	Chris Carter	Kim Manners	12 Nov 2000
8X03	Patience	Chris Carter	Chris Carter	19 Nov 2000
8X04	Roadrunners	Vince Gilligan	Rod Hardy	26 Nov 2000
8X05	Invocation	David Amann	Richard Compton	3 Dec 2000
8X06	Redrum	Steven Maeda (Story by Steven Maeda & Daniel Arkin)	Peter Markle	10 Dec 2000
8X07	Via Negativa	Frank Spotnitz	Tony Wharmby	17 Dec 2000
8X08	Surekill	Greg Walker	Terrence O'Hara	7 Jan 2001
8X09	Salvage	Jeffrey Bell	Rod Hardy	14 Jan 2001
8X10	Badlaa	John Shiban	Tony Wharmby	21 Jan 2001
8X11	The Gift	Frank Spotnitz	Kim Manners	4 Feb 2001
8X12	Medusa	Frank Spotnitz	Richard Compton	11 Feb 2001
8X13	Per Manum	Chris Carter & Frank Spotnitz	Kim Manners	18 Feb 2001
8X14	This Is Not Happening	Chris Carter & Frank Spotnitz	Kim Manners	25 Feb 2001
8X15	Deadalive	Chris Carter & Frank Spotnitz	Tony Wharmby	1 Apr 2001
8X16	Three Words	Chris Carter & Frank Spotnitz	Tony Wharmby	8 Apr 2001
8X17	Empedocles	Greg Walker	Barry K. Thomas	22 Apr 2001
8X18	Vienen	Steven Maeda	Rod Hardy	29 Apr 2001

8X19	Alone	Frank Spotnitz	Frank Spotnitz	6 May 2001
8X20	Essence	Chris Carter	Kim Manners	13 May 2001
8X21	Existence	Chris Carter	Kim Manners	20 May 2001

Season Nine

	Title	Writer(s)	Director	Originally Broadcast
9X01	Nothing Important Happened Today	Chris Carter & Frank Spotnitz	Kim Manners	11 Nov 2001
9X02	Nothing Important Happened Today II	Chris Carter & Frank Spotnitz	Tony Wharmby	18 Nov 2001
9X03	Dæmonicus	Frank Spotnitz	Frank Spotnitz	2 Dec 2001
9X04	4-D	Steven Maeda	Tony Wharmby	9 Dec 2001
9X05	Lord of the Flies	Thomas Schnauz	Kim Manners	16 Dec 2001
9X06	Trust No 1	Chris Carter & Frank Spotnitz	Tony Wharmby	6 Jan 2002
9X07	John Doe	Vince Gilligan	Michelle MacLaren	13 Jan 2002
9X08	Hellbound	David Amann	Kim Manners	27 Jan 2002
9X09	Provenance	Chris Carter & Frank Spotnitz	Kim Manners	3 Mar 2002
9X10	Providence	Chris Carter & Frank Spotnitz	Chris Carter	10 Mar 2002
9X11	Audrey Pauley	Steven Maeda	Kim Manners	17 Mar 2002
9X12	Underneath	John Shiban	John Shiban	31 Mar 2002

9X13	Improbable	Chris Carter	Chris Carter	7 Apr 2002
9X14	Scary Monsters	Thomas Schnauz	Dwight Little	14 Apr 2002
9X15	Jump the Shark	Vince Gilligan, John Shiban & Frank Spotnitz	Cliff Bole	21 Apr 2002
9X16	William	Chris Carter (Story by Chris Carter, David Duchovny & Frank Spotnitz)	David Duchovny	28 Apr 2002
9X17	Release	David Amann (Story by David Amann & John Shiban)	Kim Manners	5 May 2002
9X18	Sunshine Days	Vince Gilligan	Vince Gilligan	12 May 2002
9X19 9X20	The Truth	Chris Carter	Kim Manners	19 May 2002

Feature Film

Title	Writer(s)	Director	U.S. Release Date
The X-Files: I Want to Believe	Chris Carter & Frank Spotnitz	Chris Carter	24 July 2008

References

Books

Allrath, G. & Gymnich, M. (Ed.), *Narrative Strategies in Television Series*, Palgrave Macmillan, New York, 2005.
> Allrath, G., Gymnich, M. and Surkamp, C. "Introduction: Towards a Narratology of TV Series," pp. 1-46.
> Seibel, K. "'This is not happening': The Multi-layered Ontology of *The X-Files*," pp. 114-131.

Ang, I. *Desperately Seeking the Audience*, Routledge, London/New York, 1991.

Bassom, D. *Anderson + Duchovny: An Extraordinary Story*, Hamlyn, London, 1996.

Baudrillard, J. *Simulacra and Simulation* (translated by Sheila Faria Glaser), University of Michigan Press, Ann Arbor, 1994.
> Baudrillard, J. "The Implosion of Meaning in the Media," pp. 95-110.

Booker, K.M. *Strange TV: Innovative Television Series from The Twilight Zone to The X-Files*," Greenwood Press, Westport, 2002.
> Booker, K. M. "It's the Libidinal Economy, Stupid: *The X-Files* and the Politics of Postmodern Desire," pp. 121-149.

Braudy, L. & Cohen, M. (Ed.), *Film Theory & Criticism 7th Edition*, Oxford University Press, Oxford, 2009.
> Bazin, A. "Theater and Cinema" from *What Is Cinema?*, pp. 345-355.

Cornell, P., Day, M. and Topping, K. *X-Treme Possibilities: A Comprehensively Expanded Rummage Through Five Years of The X-Files*, Virgin Publishing, London, 1998.

Dale, T.M. & Foy, J.J. (Ed.), *Homer Simpson Marches on Washington – Dissent through American Popular Culture*, The University Press of Kentucky, Lexington, 2010.
> Cantor, P.A. "The Truth Is Still Out There: *The X-Files* and 9/11," pp. 75-96.

Dawkins, R. *Unweaving the Rainbow: Science, Delusions, and the Appetite for Wonder*, Mariner Books, New York, 1998.

Delasara, J. *Poplit, Popcult and The X-Files: A Critical Exploration*, Mcfarland & Company Inc. Publishers, Jefferson, 2000.

Dittmar, L. & Michaud, G. (Ed.), *From Hanoi to Hollywood: The Vietnam War in American Film*, Rutgers University Press, New Brunswick/London, 1990.
> Waller, G. A. "*Rambo*: Getting to Win This Time," pp. 113-128.

Ellis, J. *Visible Fictions: Cinema, Television, Video*, Routledge, London/New York, 1982.

Fiske, J. *Television Culture*, Routledge, New York, 2004.

Fiske, J. and Hartley, J. *Reading Television*, Methuen & Co Ltd, London, 1978.

Geraghty, L. *American Science Fiction Film and Television*, Berg, Oxford/New York, 2009.

Goldman J. *The X-Files: Book of the Unexplained* (Vol. 1) , Simon & Schuster, London, 1995.

Goldman J. *The X-Files: Book of the Unexplained* (Vol. 2), Simon & Schuster, London, 1996.

Hammond, M. & Mazdon, L. (Ed.), *The Contemporary Television Series*, Edinburgh University Press, Edinburgh, 2005.

> Johnson, C. "Quality/Cult Television: *The X-Files* and Television History," pp. 57-71.

Hurwitz, M. & Knowles, C. *The Complete X-Files: Behind the Series, the Myths, and the Movies*, Insight Editions, San Rafael, 2008.

Kowalski, D.A. (Ed.), *The Philosophy of The X-Files*, The University Press of Kentucky, Lexington, 2007.

> Flannery, R. and Louzecky, D. "Postdemocratic Society and the Truth Out There," pp. 55-76.

Kellner, D. *From 9/11 to Terror War: The Dangers of the Bush Legacy*, Rowman & Littlefield Publishers Inc., Lanham, 2003.

Kellner, D. *Media Spectacle*, Routledge, London, 2002.

> Kellner, D. "TV Spectacle – Aliens, conspiracies and biotechnology in *The X-Files*," pp. 126-160.

Kellner, D. *Cinema Wars: Hollywood Film and Politics in the Bush-Cheney Era*, Wiley-Blackwell, Oxford, 2010.

Kessenich, T. *Examinations: An Unauthorized Look at Seasons 6-9 of The X-Files*, Trafford, Victoria, 2002.

Knight, P. *Conspiracy Culture: From the Kennedy Assassination to The X-Files*, Routledge, London/New York, 2000.

Lavery, D., Hague, A. & Cartwright, M. (Ed.), *Deny All Knowledge: Reading The X-Files*, Syracuse University Press, Syracuse, 1996.

> Lavery, D., Hague, A. & Cartwright, M. "Introduction: Generation X – *The X-Files* and the Cultural Moment," pp. 1-21.
>
> Malach, M. "'I Want to Believe…in the FBI': The Special Agent and *The X-Files*," pp. 63-75.
>
> Reeves, J. L., Rodgers, M. C. & Epstein, M. "Rewriting Popularity: The Cult Files," pp. 22-35.

Lloyd, T. *Crises of Realism: Representing Experience in the British Novel, 1816-1910*, Bucknell University Press, Lewisburg, 1997.

Lowry, B. *The Truth Is Out There: The Official Guide to The X-Files Vol. 1*, HarperCollins Publishers, London, 1995.

Meisler, A. *Resist or Serve: The Official Guide to The X-Files Vol. 4*, Harper Collins, New York, 1999

Meisler, A. *The End and The Beginning: The Official Guide to The X-Files Vol. 5*, Harper Collins, New York, 2000.

Nelson, R. *TV Drama In Transition: Forms, Values and Cultural Change*, St Martin's Press, New York, 1997.

Rattigan, A. & Waddell, T. (Ed.), *Lounge Critic: The Couch Theorist's Companion*, ACMI/Latrobe University, Melbourne, 2004.

 Cunningham, S. "Jumping the Shark: Does the End of Sexual Tension Mean the End of Your Favourite TV Show?," pp. 145-159.

Sambrook, J. *The Eighteenth Century: The Intellectual and Cultural Context of English Literature 1700-1789 (Second Edition)*, Longman, London/New York, 1993.

Sanders, S.M. & Skoble, A.J. (Ed.), *The Philosophy of TV Noir*, The University Press of Kentucky, Lexington, 2008.

 Abrams, J.J. and Cooke, E.F. "Detection and the Logic of Abduction in *The X-Files*," pp. 179-200.

 Moses, M. V. "Kingdom of Darkness: Autonomy and Conspiracy in *The X-Files* and *Millennium*," pp. 203-227.

Sconce, J. *Haunted Media: Electronic Presence from Telegraphy to Television*, Duke University Press, Durham/London, 2000.

Scott, P. D. *The Road to 9/11: Wealth, Empire, and the Future of America*, University of California Press, Berkley, 2007.

Shearman, R. *Wanting to Believe: A Critical Guide to The X-Files, Millennium & The Lone Gunmen*, Mad Norwegian Press, Des Moines, 2009.

Short, S. *Cult Telefantasy Series: A Critical Analysis of The Prisoner, Twin Peaks, The X-Files, Buffy the Vampire Slayer, Lost, Heroes, Doctor Who and Star Trek*, McFarland & Company, Jefferson, 2011.

Simon, A. *The Real Science of The X-Files: Microbes, Meteorites, and Mutants*, Touchstone, New York, 2001.

Smith, A., Mason, D. & Hughes, W. (Ed.), *Fictions of Unease: The Gothic from Otranto to The X-Files*, Sulis Press, Newton Park, 2002.

 Kaye, H. "Fin-de-Siècle Fears: *The X-Files* as Contemporary Gothic," pp. 202-210.

Stam, R. *Film Theory: An Introduction*, Blackwell Publishing, Malden, 2000.

Thompson, J. B. *The Media and Modernity – A Social Theory of the Media*, Stanford University Press, Stanford, 1995.

Toplin, R. B. *History By Hollywood (Second Edition)*, University of Illinois Press, Urbana/Chicago, 2009.

White, M. *The Science of The X-Files*, Legend Books, London, 1996.

Williams, G. (Ed.), *The Gothic – Documents of Contemporary Art*, Whitechapel and The MIT Press, London/Cambridge, 2007.

 Edmundson, M. "Nightmare on Main Street: Angels, Sadomasochism and the Culture of Gothic," pp. 29-34.

Willis, S. *Portents of the Real: A Primer for Post-9/11 America*, Verso, London/New York, 2005.

Yang, S. R. (Ed.), *The X-Files and Literature: Unweaving the Story, Unraveling the Lie to Find the Truth*, Cambridge Scholars Publishing, Newcastle, 2007.
Yang, S. "Introduction: Weaving and Unweaving the Story," pp. xi-xxv.
Vest, J.P. "The Truth is Back There: *The X-Files* and Early Science Fiction," pp. 106-129.
Leslie-McCarthy, S. "*The X-Files*: Continuing the Psychic Detective Legacy," pp. 130-151.
Jones, C. "'Post-Modern Prometheus,' Postmodern Voices: *The X-Files* and Subjective Storytelling," pp. 174-193.
Argiro, T. "*The X-Files* Meets *Vineland*," pp. 269-297.
VanWinkle, M. "Tennyson's 'Tithonus' and the Exhaustion of Survival in *The X-Files*," pp. 298-311.
Speidel, S. "The Ending Is Out There," pp. 312-345.

Journal Articles

Baudrillard, J. "Precession of Simulacra" (translated by Paul Foss and Paul Patton) in *Art/Text*, No. 11 (Spring 1983), pp. 3-47.
Bellon, J. "The Strange Discourse of *The X-Files*: What It Is, What It Does, and What Is at Stake" in *Critical Studies in Mass Communication*, Vol. 16, Iss. 2 (1999), pp. 136-154.
Bosley, R.K. "Dark Matters" in *American Cinematographer*, Vol. 89, No. 8 (August 2008), pp. 26-37.
Broe, D. "Fox and Its Friends: Global Commodification and the New Cold War" in *Cinema Journal*, Vol. 43, No. 4 (Summer 2004), pp. 97-102.
Brooker, W. "Everywhere and nowhere: Vancouver, fan pilgrimage and the urban imaginary" in *International Journal of Cultural Studies*, Vol. 10, No. 4 (2007), pp. 423-444.
Brown, S. "Memento Mori: The Slow Death of *The X-Files*" in *Science Fiction Film & Television*, Vol. 6, Issue 1 (2013), pp. 7-22.
Burns, C. "Erasure: Alienation, Paranoia and the Loss of Memory in *The X-Files*" in *Camera Obscura* 45, Vol.15, No.3 (2001), pp. 195-224.
Campbell, J.E. "Alien(ating) ideology and the American media: Apprehending the alien image in television through *The X-Files*" in *International Journal of Cultural Studies*, Vol. 4, No. 3 (2001), pp. 327-347.
Corner, J. "Presumption as Theory: 'Realism' in Television Studies" in *Screen*, Vol. 33, No. 1 (Spring 1992), pp. 97-102.
Dorsey, L.G. "Re-Reading *The X-Files*: The Trickster in Contemporary Conspiracy Myth" in *Western Journal of Communication*, Vol. 66, No. 4 (Fall 2002), pp. 448-468.
Fiske, J. "Popular Narrative and Commercial Television" in *Camera Obscura* 23, Vol. 8, No. 2 (May 1990), pp. 133-147.

Haggins, B.L. "Apocrypha Meets *The Pentagon Papers:* The Appeals of *The X-Files* to the X-Phile" in *Journal of Film and Video*, Vol. 53, No. 4 (Winter 2001/2002), pp. 8-28.

Howley, K. "Spooks, Spies, and Control Technology in *The X-Files*" in *Television & New Media*, Vol. 2, No. 3 (August 2001), pp. 257-280.

Kelley-Romano, S. "Trust No One: The Conspiracy Genre on American Television" in *The Southern Communication Journal*, Vol. 73, No. 2 (April-June 2008), pp. 105-121.

Kellner, D. "*The X-Files* and the Aesthetics and Politics of Postmodern Pop" in *The Journal of Aesthetics and Art Criticism*, Vol. 57, No. 2 (Spring 1999), pp. 161-175.

Kellner, D. "*The X-Files*, Paranoia, and Conspiracy: From the 70s to the 90s" in *Framework*, Vol. 41 (Fall 1999), pp. 16-36.

Kinney, K. "*The X-Files* and the Borders of the Post-Cold War World" in *Journal of Film and Video*, Vol. 53, No. 4 (Winter 2001/2002), pp. 54-71.

Kompare, D. "Publishing Flow: DVD Box Sets and the Reconception of Television" in *Television & New Media*, Vol. 7, No. 4 (November 2006), pp. 335-360.

Kruse, A. "*The X-Files*: Entries on Meaning" in *Sydney Studies in English*, Vol. 23 (1997), pp. 108-134.

Kydd, E. "Differences: *The X-Files*, Race and the White Norm" in *Journal of Film and Video*, Vol. 53, No. 4 (Winter 2001/2002), pp. 72-82.

Markley, R. "Alien Assassinations: *The X-Files* and the Paranoid Structure of History" in *Camera Obscura* 40-41, Vol. 14, No. 1-2 (May 1997), pp. 77-102.

McLean, A. "Marshall McLuhan, Television Culture, and '*The X-Files*'" in *Film Quarterly*, Vol. 51, No. 4 (Summer 1998), pp. 2-11.

Milner, A. "Postmodern Gothic: *Buffy*, *The X-Files* and the Clinton Presidency" in *Continuum: Journal of Media & Cultural Studies*, Vol. 19, No. 1 (March 2005), pp. 103-116.

Mittell, J. "Narrative Complexity in Contemporary American Television" in *The Velvet Light Trap*, No. 58 (Fall 2006), pp. 29-40.

Morris, M. "The truth is out there…" in *Australian Book Review*, No. 181 (June 1996), pp. 17-20.

Neumann, A.W. "*The X-Files* and the Longing for Belief" in *Quadrant*, Vol. 40, No. 9 (September 1996), pp. 23-27.

Picarelli, E. & Gomez-Galisteo, M. C. "Be fearful – *The X-Files*' post 9/11 legacy" in *Science Fiction Film & Television*, Vol. 6, Issue 1 (2013), pp.71-85.

Ramirez, J. and Olsen, S.D. "X-Philes: Imaginations of Millenial Anxieties" in *Journal of Film and Video*, Vol. 53, No. 4 (Winter 2001/2002), pp. 3-7.

Scodari, C. & Felder, J.L. "Creating a Pocket Universe: 'Shippers,' Fan Fiction, and *The X-Files* Online" in *Communication Studies*, Vol. 51, No. 3 (Fall 2000), pp. 238-257.

Soukup, C. "Television Viewing as Vicarious Resistance: *The X-Files* and Conspiracy Discourse" in *The Southern Communication Journal*, Vol. 68, No. 1 (Fall 2002), pp. 14-26.

Westerfelhaus, R. & Combs, T. A. "Criminal Investigations and Spiritual Quests: The X-Files as an Example of Hegemonic Concordance in a Mass-Mediated Society" in *Journal of Communication Inquiry*, Vol. 22, No. 2 (April 1998), pp. 205-220.

Wooley, C.A. "Visible Fandom: Reading *The X-Files* Through X-Philes" in *Journal of Film and Video*, Vol. 53, No. 4 (Winter 2001/2002), pp. 29-53.

Magazine/Newspaper Articles

Adalian, J. "Twentieth renews off-net '*X-Files*'in 135 markets," *Daily Variety Gotham*, 25 September 2000, p. 3.

Barr, M. "*The X-Files* Revivial Isn't About Fans Or Closure, It's About Net-flix," *Forbes*, 24 March 2015. Retrieved from:
> http://www.forbes.com/sites/merrillbarr/2015/03/24/x-files-reboot/ (accessed 23 September 2015).

Denton, A. "*X-Files*: An Investigation" in *Rolling Stone*, Issue 517 (Yearbook 1995), pp. 67-74.

Flint, J, "It's Fox vs Fox" in *Entertainment Weekly*, Issue 501 (3 Sep 1999), pp.15-16.

Kaufman, A. "An 'X-Files' Mystery; Film Will Reveal Whether Fox Can Revive Aging Cult Favorite" in *The Wall Street Journal* (Easter Edition), New York, 25 July 2008, p. B12.

Kissell, R. "When the Flame Flickers Out" in *Daily Variety*, Vol. 291, No. 42 (31 May 2006), p. A8.

Lipsky, D. "Chris Carter in the Virtue of Paranoia" in *Rolling Stone*, Iss. 533 (March 1997), pp. 47-50, 111.

Millman, J. "*The X-Files* Finds the Truth: It's Time is Past" in *The New York Times*, 19 May 2002. Retrieved from:
> http://www.nytimes.com/2002/05/19/arts/television-radio-the-x-files-finds-the-truth-its-time-is-past.html
> (accessed 29 September 2010).

Persons, D. "The Making of X-Cops" in *Cinefantastique*, Vol. 32, Iss. 3 (October 2000), pp. 28-29.

Pinaire, B.K. "Skeptical Opinions: Internet Conspiracies" in *Skeptic*, Vol. 12, No. 1 (2005), p. 26.

Roberts, J.L. "TV Turns Vertical" in *Newsweek*, Vol. 132, Iss. 16 (19 October 1998), p. 54.

Vitaris, P. "Academic X-Philes" in *Cinefantastaique*, Vol. 28, Iss. 3 (October 1996), pp. 21-22, 62.

Vitaris, P. "*The X-Files: Fight the Future* (Review)" in *Cinefantastique*, Vol. 30, No. 7/8 (October 1998), p. 51, 124.
Vitaris, P. and Coyle, D. "X'd Out" in *Cinefantastique*, Vol. 34, Iss. 2 (April 2002), pp. 38-41.
Wild, D. "*X-Files*: Undercover" in *Rolling Stone*, Issue 524 (July 1996), pp. 54-58, 97.
Wolcott, J. "'X' Factor" in *The New Yorker*, Vol. 70, Iss. 9 (April 18 1994), pp. 98-99.
Wolcott, J. "Too Much Pulp" in *The New Yorker*, Vol. 72, Iss.41 (6 January 1997), pp. 76-77.

Films
(in order of production)

Rope (1948), Writ. Arthur Laurents, Dir. Alfred Hitchcock, Warner Bros/Transatlantic Pictures/Universal.
Rashomon (1950), Writ. Akira Kurosawa & Shinobu Hashimoto, Dir. Akira Kurosawa, Daiei Film Co. Ltd.
Klute (1971), Writ. Andy Lewis & Dave Lewis, Dir. Alan Pakula, Warner Bros/Gus Productions.
Star Wars (1977), Writ. George Lucas, Dir. George Lucas, Twentieth Century Fox/Lucasfilm.
JFK (1991), Writ. Oliver Stone & Zachary Sklar (story by Jim Garrison & Jim Marrs), Dir. Oliver Stone, Warner Bros/Studio Canal/Regency Enterprises/Alcor Films/Ixtlan Corporation.
The X-Files: Fight the Future (1998), Writ. Chris Carter (story by Chris Carter & Frank Spotnitz), Dir. Rob Bowman, Twentieth Century Fox/ Ten Thirteen.
The X-Files: I Want to Believe (2008), Writ. Chris Carter & Frank Spotnitz, Dir. Chris Carter, Twentieth Century Fox/Ten Thirteen.
The Hobbit: An Unexpected Journey (2012), Writ. Fran Walsh, Philippa Boyens, Peter Jackson & Guillermo del Toro, Dir. Peter Jackson, New Line Cinema/Metro Goldwyn Mayer/Wingnut Films/Warner Bros.

Television Series
(in order of production)

American Broadcasting Company, *The Brady Bunch*, 1969 – 1974, Paramount Television.
CBS Broadcasting, *The Waltons*, 1972 – 1981, Lorimar Productions.
Twentieth Century Fox, *The Simpsons*, 1989 – present, Gracie Films.

Twentieth Century Fox/Spike, *Cops*, 1989 – present, Barbour/Langley Productions/Fox Television Stations/Langley Productions/Spike Original Productions.
Multimedia Entertainment/NBC Universal, *The Jerry Springer Show*, 1991 – present, Stamford Media Center Productions.
Twentieth Century Fox, *The X-Files*, 1993 – 2002, Ten Thirteen.
Twentieth Century Fox, *Millennium*, 1996 – 1999, Ten Thirteen.
Twentieth Century Fox, *The Lone Gunmen*, 2001, Ten Thirteen.
Twentieth Century Fox, *24*, 2001 – 2010, Imagine Entertainment.
AMC, *Breaking Bad*, 2008 – 2013, High Bridge Entertainment/Gran Via Productions/Sony Pictures Television.

DVDs

The X-Files: The Complete Sixth Season, Region 4, Twentieth Century Fox Home Entertainment, 2002, DVD.
The X-Files: The Complete Ninth Season, Region 4, Twentieth Century Fox Home Entertainment, 2004, DVD.
The X-Files Mythology: Super Soldiers, Region 1, Twentieth Century Fox Home Entertainment, 2005, DVD.
The X-Files - Essentials, Region 4, Twentieth Century Fox Home Entertainment, 2008, DVD.

Internet References

Archive of American Television, "Interview – Vince Gilligan," 9 August 2011. Retrieved from:
    http://www.emmytvlegends.org/interviews/people/vince-gilligan# (accessed 23 September 2015).
Box Office Mojo, "The X-Files." Retrieved from:
    http://www.boxofficemojo.com/movies/?id=x-filesfightthefuture.htm (accessed 25 November 2015).
Box Office Mojo, "The X-Files: I Want to Believe." Retrieved from:
    http://www.boxofficemojo.com/movies/?id=xfiles2.htm (accessed 25 November 2015).
Fox, J. D. "What The Critics Are Saying About *The Hobbit's* High Frame Rate," *Vulture*, 14 December 2012. Retrieved from:
    http://www.vulture.com/2012/12/critics-on-the-hobbits-high-frame-rate.html# (accessed 23 September 2015).
Gallup, "Presidential Approval Ratings – George W. Bush," 21-22 September 2001. Retrieved from:

http://www.gallup.com/poll/116500/Presidential-Approval-Ratings-George-Bush.aspx (accessed 15 September 2010).

Goodman, T. "*X-Files'* creator ends Fox series," *San Francisco Chronicle*, 18 January 2002. Retrieved from:

http://www.sfgate.com/entertainment/article/X-Files-creator-ends-Fox-series-2883631.php (accessed 23 September 2015).

President George H.W. Bush, Remarks at the Annual Convention of the National Religious Broadcasters, Sheraton Washington Hotel, Washington D.C. 27 January 1992. Retrieved from:

http://bushlibrary.tamu.edu/research/public_papers.php?id=3882&year=1992&month=01 (accessed 15 September 2010).

President Ronald Reagan, Remarks at the National Association of Evangelicals, Sheraton Twin Towers Hotel, Orlando, Florida, 8 March 1983. Retrieved from:

http://www.reagan.utexas.edu/archives/speeches/1983/30883b.htm (accessed 26 September 2010).

ABOUT THE AUTHOR

M. A. Crang is an avid fan of *The X-Files*.
He holds a Bachelor of Arts, with first class Honours in Film & Television
Studies. His passions include movies, jogging and travelling.
He currently lives with his wife in Japan.

www.ingramcontent.com/pod-product-compliance
Lightning Source LLC
Chambersburg PA
CBHW030702190526
45164CB00004B/119